D1034809

JUDAISM

IS VOLUME

73

OF THE

Twentieth Century Encyclopedia of Catholicism

UNDER SECTION

VI

THE WORD OF GOD

IT IS ALSO THE

72ND

VOLUME IN ORDER OF PUBLICATION

Edited by HENRI DANIEL-ROPS of the Académie Française

JUDAISM

by PAUL DÉMANN

Translated from the French by P. J. HEPBURNE-SCOTT

HAWTHORN BOOKS · PUBLISHERS · *New York*

 This book is manufactured in the United States of America and was published simultaneously in Canada by McClelland & Stewart, Ltd., 25 Hollinger Rd., Toronto 16. It was originally published in France under the title *Les Juifs, foi et destinée,* © Librairie Arthème Fayard, 1960. The Library of Congress has catalogued The Twentieth Century Encyclopedia of Catholicism under card number 58-14327. Library of Congress card number for this volume: 61-15611. The Catholic University of America Library has catalogued this volume under the Lynn-Peterson Alternative Classification for Catholic Books: BQT184.T9v.73/BM640. Dewey decimal classification: 296.

First Edition, August, 1961

NIHIL OBSTAT

Joannes M. T. Barton, S.T.D., L.S.S.

Censor deputatus

IMPRIMATUR

E. Morrogh Bernard

Vicarius Generalis

Westmonasterii, die XIX JUNIS, MCMLXI

The Nihil Obstat and Imprimatur are a declaration that a book or pamphlet is considered to be free from doctrinal or moral error. It is not implied that those who have granted the Nihil obstat and Imprimatur agree with the contents, opinions or statements expressed.

CONTENTS

NOTE ON RENDERING OF HEBREW WORDS

The spellings of the Hebrew names and words in this book do not follow any of the scientific methods, in which every Hebrew letter has its precise equivalent in our type. These involve special typographical symbols which can only bewilder and distract the reader unfamiliar with Hebrew. The spellings here adopted follow conventions in common use among English-speaking Jews, and give a rough guide to pronunciation. In this connection, it should be noted that the letters *ch* are pronounced approximately as in the Scots "loch", not as in "charity" or in "character".

Translations of official prayers are taken from Singer's *Authorised Daily Prayer Book of the United Hebrew Congregations of the British Empire;* London, Eyre and Spottiswoode, 26th edition, 1960.

INTRODUCTION

The position of this volume in this series is alone suggestive of a programme. Thirty years ago this book on Judaism would certainly have been included in the section devoted to non-Christian beliefs, but today it seems perfectly natural to include the Jews among the "separated brethren", as indeed Pius XII did in his 1950 Christmas message. From the outset, then, the Christian reader's attention is drawn to the fundamental relationship between Judaism and Christianity, between Israel and the Church. Parted from us by the earliest and saddest of all separations, the Jews are nonetheless not strangers but our brethren, by a very special title, and indeed our "elder brethren", our "elders in the faith" (the original suggestion for the title of this book). They are still truly members of Israel, of that Israel of the Bible, which is the root from which we spring. Their destiny and their faith, moreover, as well as their existence in our midst, are of the deepest concern to ourselves. That is the essential justification of this book.

But first we must clear up a question, obviously complex and too often obscured by confusions and misunderstandings: what is it we are to discuss? Who are "the Jews" of our title? Who are these twelve million people, whom they and others alike call Jews, some of whom are believers, some unbelievers, some black, some white, some rich, some poor, some English, others French, Russians, Brazilians, Ethiopians, etc.? What have they in common? What distinguishes them from others? Above all, what does their presence in the world signify, especially for the Christian?

They are no myth: they exist. They are men like everyone

else. But for us, by clear historical continuity, they represent above all the people of the Exodus, of the Covenant, of the Bible, the people of Abraham, Moses, David, Isaias—the people, too, of Jesus, of Mary, of Peter, John and Paul—whereas many ancient peoples of biblical days have long since disappeared from the stage of history.

Are they descendants by blood, for what that is worth, of the ancient Hebrews? Are they a race apart, as some have often imagined, and even tried to prove, by constructing a whole false science to serve unacknowledged passions or interests? The verdict of both history and biology is definite: numerous admixtures and widespread proselytism, from their origins onwards—in Canaan, the whole Near East, the Mediterranean basin, North Africa, Spain, Russia, etc.—have made the Jews, like most human groupings, a regular mosaic. The traits of physiognomy, psychology or mentality which seem characteristic and fairly stable for the Jews of a particular milieu or locality (though too often generalized by ignorance or prejudice) are not hereditary, but the products of particular historical situations, the products of an often very penetrating human and spiritual climate, transmitted by the influence of the milieu, by education, by the constant experience of a shared condition, but also modified when the milieu and the condition are transformed. Further, the clear conclusions of historical and scientific research, and observation of certain parts of the Jewish world, now in a state of rapid development, enable us to obtain some experimental verification of these statements. This is particularly true of the unprecedented experiment now before the eyes of the world in the State of Israel, where year by year we can see how a new people is being formed, with physical and mental characteristics often markedly different from those of their forebears, out of pioneers and survivors from the most diverse Jewish communities of eighty different countries.

Must we then say that the Jews constitute, if not a race, then a people? Certainly that was true for two or even three thousand years. In the unification and development of this people its faith and the consciousness of its mission no doubt played a determining part, but it never had, and still less did it keep, all the characteristics of a people. When the little Jewish State (which at the time of Christ still harboured about a quarter of the Jews of that time) had finally succumbed, the scattered Jewish communities, while sharing as far as possible in the life and culture of their surroundings, preserved not only their loyalty to their faith and tradition but also their consciousness and characteristics as a people, all through the Middle Ages. But when the French Revolution decreed the civic emancipation of the Jews and thus put an end to the peculiar status of their communities, it gave birth to an evolution which profoundly transformed the situation of Jewry. Mingling in the life and activities of different peoples, very many Jews are now being integrated and progressively assimilated to their national culture and life. By this very fact, and to the extent that this evolution has taken place, the Jews cease to constitute a people apart.

Since 1948, indeed, we have been witnessing the rebirth of a Jewish nation, the Israeli nation, in the framework of the State of Israel. But it is now all the more evident that the great majority of some ten million Jews dispersed throughout the world consider themselves English, French, Russian, American, Argentinian, etc., and in spite of their legitimate and active sympathy with the State of Israel they are nowise inclined to confuse their Jewish loyalty with their loyalty to their nation.

If they are neither a race nor a people, in the ordinary sense of the word, can the Jews be defined simply as the followers of a religion, of the Jewish faith? Is one, for instance, simply a French Jew (or Israelite), as one may be a French Catholic or Protestant? There are Jews who believe little or nothing, or who are not even circumcised, or who, being born of a non-Jewish mother, do not count as Jews in Jewish religious law; yet these no less feel and consider themselves Jews, and are no less considered so by the others. Membership of Judaism is a reality of a different nature from membership of any other confession, something more complex and difficult to define.

What does it mean, then, to be a Jew? Perhaps the least inadequate answer would be something like this: to be a Jew is to belong to a community with a special destiny, which is defined only by history, and this unique history and destiny, with the concrete human condition which flows from them, are closely bound up with the Bible history (the history of salvation, in the eyes of the believer). With some, this "belonging" will be expressed by loyalty to the tradition of Judaism and the conscious acceptance of a destiny founded on divine election; in others it will take the form of an attachment, whether willing and accepted or almost instinctive, and of a feeling of solidarity, founded on a common descent, tradition, education and condition. Clearly, then, there are several ways of being a Jew, but this does not prevent the Jews from forming an entity whose cohesion, permanence and "personality" stand out with extraordinary vigour.

What are we to call this complex reality? "Judaism" stands rather for the Jewish religion, its doctrine, tradition and practice.[1] "The Jewish people" is not wholly appropriate, as we have seen, since the Jews no longer constitute a "people" in the ordinary, secular sense of the word. Its use would be justified rather in a religious context (as we also speak of the "Christian people"), where it would designate the historic community of Judaism as a unit in the history of salvation. The name "Israel", which in biblical times at first denoted the Northern Kingdom as distinct from Juda, but later became the supreme religious name for the people of God, is also patent of two other interpretations. In Christian theology tradition applies this name equally and above all to the Church, and in the secular context the name is now borne

[1] The word "Jewry", though a little antique in flavour, can well be used for the Jewish community as a whole, especially in a particular country or area. It is frequently so used in *The Jewish Encyclopaedia.* (*Trans.*)

by a national State, the State of Israel. Even the word "Jew" is not free of a certain ambiguity. Not to mention those distortions by which, in several languages, under the weight of age-old prejudices, the word has been given offensive and malicious meanings, we may use the word "Jews" to denote sometimes all those who belong to the historic community of the Jewish "people", sometimes only those Jews who are faithful to their belief and tradition, who really represent "Judaism" as a religion. (We find the same ambiguity in the use of the word "Christian" by non-Christians, and sometimes even by Christians.)

However, if we are to treat of our subject at all, we are obliged to use these different terms, for there are no others at our disposal. These remarks, however, together with the context in which the terms appear, should suffice to prevent confusion and give a sufficiently precise meaning to our observations.

The complexity of these questions of terminology merely reflects the complexity of our subject. That is why we cannot rest content with a simple explanation of the main lines of the faith, tradition and practice of Judaism. To obtain some grasp of Judaism in all its actual dimensions, we shall have to place the exposition of the Jewish religion in its historical context, which is not simply that of the development of a religion, but also that of the destiny and historical condition of a people. Moreover, we shall not be able, as Christians, to understand the meaning of this great fact of Israel—which touches us very closely—unless we place it not only in its historical context but also in its theological perspective, in our Christian vision of the history of salvation.

As this last is the most fundamental for us, it will be logical to begin with it. After a first chapter designed to give a Christian understanding of Israel's destiny, we shall briefly sketch the historical facts which are indispensable to an understanding of the life and tradition of Judaism in the past and the present. With these foundations laid, we shall then be able to outline a general view of the Jewish religion, in its essential, permanent and present features. With such a vast subject, our treatment of it will inevitably be summary, but we hope it will not be over-simplified. We shall avoid all excessive erudition, which would be out of place here. We shall try not to swamp the reader with masses of data or encyclopedic knowledge, but to help him to penetrate, to understand Judaism, its historical condition and its problems, its underlying structure, its inspiration, its soul. This penetration, this understanding, are clearly not a matter of knowledge alone. A community, a destiny, a religion, are not understood without deep sympathy and a certain fellow-feeling. The fundamental kinship, the profound solidarity, which bind the Christian to Israel, should be enough to create these conditions of brotherly understanding. A long and unhappy history, woven of conflicts, tragedies and miseries, has worked for centuries to destroy these conditions. But now a happy evolution is tending to restore to Christians of our time that openmindedness and that desire for a respectful and brotherly approach which—in spite of all that separates us—puts us in a better position to understand the life and tradition of Judaism. It is to those Christians of our day who are ready for this effort that this little book is dedicated.

CHAPTER I

ISRAEL AND THE CHURCH

THE CHRISTIAN VIEW OF ISRAEL'S DESTINY

The people of God in the Old Testament

For the Church, as for Israel, the Old Testament is God's Word, Revelation, the history of salvation, and that on the same title-deeds as the New Testament. It is first of all in the Old Testament that we find God's design for his people revealed, a design clearly displayed from the beginning of biblical history, with the call of Abraham. In order to speak to men, to reveal himself to them, to redeem them from sin and to unite them in a single people of God, God began by calling and setting apart a man, with his family, and his posterity: Israel. To this people he progressively revealed himself through his envoys the prophets, as the true God, the only God, the living God, the Saviour-God. It was this divine choice that creates the people of Israel. It was after the first great intervention of the Saviour-God, the deliverance of the Hebrews from the slavery of Egypt, that the twelve tribes, through the Covenant of Sinai, became truly a nation and came to realize that they were God's people, the bearer of his message, his promises and the pledges of his loving tenderness in the midst of the nations, and also *for* the nations. To train Israel for the performance of its mission and to protect the purity of the revelation entrusted to it, God gave Israel an exclusive law of life, separating it from other peoples, and this separation became deeply engraven on Israel's soul, on its history and that of its relations with other nations. But the ultimate aim of this setting apart of a "kingdom of priests" (Exod. 19. 6) is the salvation of all men. In God's designs, Israel represents all mankind. Israel is his witness. The dialogue of Israel with its Lord, the story of its loyalties and disloyalties, is the story of every man, of every one of us.

Like the Church herself today, Israel "holds this treasure in earthen vessels" (2 Cor. 4. 7): it is by accomplishing his work of salvation in spite of the pettiness and frailties of his chosen instrument that God shows forth the mercy and free bounty of his gifts, his faithfulness to his promises, against which no human unfaithfulness can prevail (Rom. 3. 3). At every stage of his people's pilgrimage God thus keeps for himself at least a "remnant" (Deut. 4. 7; Isaias 1. 9; 6. 13; 17. 5–6; Soph. 3. 12, etc.) and handful of men "who have not bowed the knee to Baal" (3 Kings 19. 18; cf. Rom. 11. 4), through whom the realization of his designs is to be carried out. But the object of his election and his love is always the whole chosen people, and beyond the people it is all mankind, whom in the end he will gather and bring back to himself. All the vicissitudes of the history of God's people and its purifying trials have no other object but this (Osee 2. 8–9; 5. 15; 11. 8–9; Amos 9. 11–14; Deut. 30. 1–5, etc.).

To the Jews, this history is still going on, without a break. To the Christian, it reveals a design of grace, which yet is paradoxical and prepares the way for reverses which humanly are quite unpredictable, but it is also a design of divine faithfulness; it is unthinkable that God should forsake that people (and not simply its individual members) which, on behalf of all the others, had received the promises and pledges of his love, or that he should exclude this people from his designs: "With unchanging love I love thee, and now in mercy I have drawn thee to myself" (Jer. 31. 3); "I will never cast away the seed of Jacob, and of David my servant" (Jer. 35. 25–6).

The drama of God's people in the Gospels

The key to a Christian view of Israel's destinies is found in the New Testament, above all in the Gospels, not so much in the explanations to be found there as in the actual events they record.

All the successive interventions of God and all the faithful acts of Israel in the days of the Old Covenant culminate in Jesus Christ and find in him and his work their first realization, complete, yet continuing, for their total and final realization is only to be achieved at the end of his work, in the Second Coming. But the decisive days of the first coming of Jesus the Christ (that is, the Messiah) did not pass without a drama which at first sight is disconcerting. Perfectly human, a Jew of his day, a descendant of Abraham, a new Moses, son of David, heir of the prophets, friend of "the poor", imbued with all the tradition of Israel, Jesus is in perfect continuity with his people and its history. We can understand nothing of his teaching or of that of his disciples, if we do not place it in that Jewish setting, in the context of the living tradition of Israel or, worse, if we oppose it to that tradition. But at the same time, by his Godhead he transcends time, history and every earthly thing. In that respect, he is in discontinuity with the history which prepared his coming. He perfectly fulfils the mission and expectation of Israel, but he also surpasses all that was limited and provisional in them, radically transforming their outlook and proportions. Faced with him, the sons of Abraham are called to make a new act of faith: the acceptance, however difficult, of the novelty of a Messiah who is a God-Man, a Messiah crucified and risen; the acceptance too of a profound transformation of the people of God, rising above the received traditions and institutions, the provisional limitations, the exclusiveness inherent in the condition of the people of the Old Covenant.

This step, easier for the "poor of Israel", for the humble, even for the sinners, was harder for those who had the duty of preserving the spiritual and national heritage of the chosen people, those who felt the responsibilities and also the temptations of power, whether spiritual or political, the "pious", the doctors, the high priests, the notables dependent on the

Roman conquerors. According to the Gospels, the opposition to Jesus and finally his condemnation and handing over to the Roman authority were the work of a group of religious and political leaders, whereas the mass of the people of Judaea and Galilee who could understand Jesus' teaching showed themselves, on the whole, in his favour. Easily roused to enthusiasm, though often incapable of understanding the real bearing of his words, they were, like all popular masses, fickle and readily influenced. It was at first from their ranks, and only later from the ruling classes, that the apostles and disciples were drawn, and the primitive Christian community was formed. Thus, by the decisive choice in face of the Christ, the chosen people was shown to be the exemplar and representative of all mankind, its destinies to be of universal and permanent significance.

By these events a profound rupture, a *schism*, was produced in the heart of the people of God, between the "remnant" which held to Christ and was soon to appear as a distinct community, and the rest of the people, in whose eyes this new community would soon appear, fatally, as a heretical sect. The Christian community, on its side, quickly became aware of the universal import of the mystery and the message of Christ and opened its doors wide, without restriction, to the heathen, to the Gentiles, many of whom were already strongly attracted by the religion of Israel, without always going so far as to become members of its community. This is another paradoxical aspect of the plan of salvation: those who seemed the best prepared, the children of Israel, in some ways found more difficulty in accepting Christ and his Gospel than those who were "far away", "strangers to the covenants of the promise, without hope and without God in the world" (Ephes. 2. 12). Thus was fulfilled a saying which was a sort of *leitmotiv* in the teaching of Jesus: "the first shall be last and the last shall be first". The rapid and soon numerous conversions from among the Gentiles compelled the Church to realize which elements in the Jewish tradition were only provisional and peculiar to the Jews, and thus hastened the abandonment of the "observances" of the Law, and this very fact decisively emphasized the break between the two communities.

But in spite of this break and the lamentable conflict resulting from it, the Church preserves the consciousness of her essential solidarity with Israel. The Church, the "remnant" of Israel (enlarged by the entry of the Gentiles, now become sons of Abraham by faith), knows that she is called to reunite Jews and Gentiles in her bosom. It is not a substitution of one people for another, but a transformation and universalizing of the same people of God, now come to the fullness of its vocation.

This transformation and this break were foreseen in the first three Gospels, but could not appear there clearly, for the good reason that their narratives were confined to the personal work and teaching of Jesus, in the Palestinian Jewish setting in which he lived, and to the time when the tragedy of the break between the young Christian community and the Jewish world around it had not yet finally occurred.

The Gospel according to St John, compiled at the end of the first century, when the separation between the two communities was an accomplished fact, did not attempt to explain its historical development, but rather to teach its "typical", permanent and universal theological significance.[1]

The mystery of Israel in the thought of St Paul

It was given to Paul, the former Pharisee, appointed Apostle of the Gentiles, to grasp and expound both the tragic, baffling nature of the drama and its true significance

[1] This characteristic attitude of St John's Gospel has often been lost sight of, when a concrete and historical sense has been given to expressions which he uses in a theological and "typical" sense, as for instance when he speaks of "the Jews", obviously meaning, not the Jews in general, but the enemies of Jesus, the hostile leaders, excluding the people, or even in contrast to the people (for example, in 7. 11–13, etc.).

in the designs of God. He pondered it deeply in the light of Scripture and tradition, in the light of Christ crucified and risen, and of his own vocation and apostolic experience.

In the history of Israel Paul is thus led to distinguish two planes: that of the dispensation of the promise and of faith, which is permanent and universal, beginning historically with the call of Abraham and finding its fulfilment in Christ, and that of the Law which, because of sin and in view of redemption, separates Israel from the nations, thus making a division which is essentially temporary, meant for the time of preparation for the Messiah (Gal. 3; Rom. 4).[2] To Paul, Christ takes that central place which in Judaism was occupied by the *Torah*, the Law, the inclusive expression of the whole Jewish religion. He is the first to proclaim clearly that the pagans who come to Christ are not obliged to submit to the "observances" of the Law; Christ alone suffices to justify those who believe in him. This alone establishes the principle that the observances of the Law are abrogated, even for the Jews who have come to believe in Christ. Thus between the two communities arose a controversy which, in the course of centuries, took the form of an opposition between Christ and the Law, the Christians reproaching the Jews with rejecting Christ, the Jews reproaching the Christians with rejecting the Law.

But now that the Christ has come and the redemption has been accomplished, the division between Israel and the nations was to have come to an end. By his cross, the Redeemer must have overthrown the wall which had separated "the two peoples", in order to reunite them in one, in one single body (Ephes. 2. 11–18), so that finally, as to the *religious* destinies of mankind, there should be "no more Gentile and Jew, . . . nothing but Christ in any of us" (Col.

[2] St Paul also makes it clear that this distinction concerns the course of the history of salvation and not the essential conditions of personal salvation, for every man, Jew or Gentile, is judged, from this point of view, solely according to his lights and his conscience (cf. Rom. 1–3).

3. 11). This vision of unity corresponds to a fundamental aspect of redemption. God's design is one. It is sin which has broken the unity and harmony of creation by dividing man from God and from himself, men from each other and man from the universe. Redemption will not be complete till the day when the unity and harmony of God's work is wholly re-established. Now since the greater part of the chosen people, with its representative institutions, has remained outside the Church of Christ, the reunion of the two peoples has been nullified, or at least retarded, which for Paul is the cause of "great sorrow and unceasing grief" (Rom. 9. 2). He comes to understand, however, that so far from frustrating the divine plan—of the dispensation of grace and the cross—this apparent obstacle is perfectly integrated with it.

At the same time, the providential bearing of the fact that a great part of Israel remains outside forces itself as an objective fact on the apostle's experience and reflection. The resistance offered by Israel turns the primitive Church towards the evangelization of the Gentiles, and helps it to realize the implications of its catholicity (Rom. 11. 12–15).

Moreover, the "lapse" is only partial. In its "remnant", Israel has accomplished its mission. Paul himself, with the whole primitive community, is witness to that. By her continuity with the Israel which was faithful to the former Covenant, the Church bears witness to God's fidelity to his promise (Rom. 11. 1–4, 17–24).

What, then, is the condition and meaning of Israel, separated from the Church? Israel, St Paul replies, is neither entirely nor finally in disgrace: "God has not disowned his people" (Rom. 11. 2). "In the preaching of the gospel, God rejects them, . . . but in his elective purpose he still welcomes them, for the sake of their fathers (*i.e.*, the patriarchs); God does not repent of the gifts he makes, or of the calls he issues" (Rom. 11. 28–9). "Some, to be sure, showed unfaithfulness on their side, but can we suppose that unfaithfulness on their side will dispense God from his promises?" (Rom. 3. 3).

Yet if God preserves his love for Israel, how are we to understand its persistent separation? The lapse of nineteen centuries, together with the spectacle of the providential preservation of the Jewish people through countless vicissitudes, makes this question still more urgent for us. True, the Apostle assures us that "the result of their false step has been to bring the Gentiles salvation", that "their false step has enriched the world" (Rom. 11. 11–12): but was Israel somehow to be sacrificed for the benefit of the Gentile Church, as a mistaken apologetic has sometimes supposed? Far from it: "Have they stumbled, so as to fall altogether? God forbid it!" he cries (Rom. 11. 12). This is the *mystery*—the hidden plan God wishes to reveal to us—the mystery which St Paul would have all the nations know, "or else you might have too good a conceit of yourselves" (Rom. 11. 16–24): "Blindness has fallen upon a part of Israel, but only until the tale of the Gentile nations is complete; then the whole of Israel shall find salvation" (Rom. 11. 25–7). This reintegration of Israel will gloriously show forth God's faithfulness and mercy, and St Paul ascribes to it immense importance in the history of salvation: "If their false step has enriched the world . . . what must we expect, when it is made good? . . . If the losing of them has meant a world reconciled to God, what can the winning of them mean, but life risen from the dead?" (Rom. 11. 12–15). This certitude, which St Paul places at the very centre of the Christian hope, is for us the key to the destiny of the Jewish people.

To the Christian, it is in the light of this hope that the providential preservation and presence of the Jewish people receive all their positive significance.[3] And it is in the light of this hope that the Church, in the last resort, defines her theological attitude to Judaism.

[3] Nothing could be more foreign to St Paul's teaching than to interpret the sufferings of the Jewish people in the course of history as signs of reprobation, or even a curse, by twisting certain New Testament texts (e.g. Matt. 27. 25) out of their true meaning.

OUTLINE OF THE HISTORY OF JEWISH-CHRISTIAN RELATIONS

In the last section we spoke of the initial rupture. Between the two separated communities, now living side by side, at first in Palestine and then throughout the Diaspora[4] of the Mediterranean and the East, there was inevitably opposition, conflict, rivalry. Each sprang from the one root and claimed the same patrimony, the Scriptures. Each was convinced of being the people of God, the "true Israel", heir of the promises, steward of revelation. To the Church, the certitude of this continuity lay in her faith in Christ, himself the fulfilment of the Scriptures and of Israel's whole history. For Judaism there was the tangible evidence of the continuity of its tradition and institutions, of all its religious and national life. Their respective claims were mutually contradictory and it was equally vital for either to stake out and justify its claims against the other. Moreover, with regard to the pagan world, an undying rivalry arose between the preaching of the Gospel and Jewish proselytizing, which was very active during the early Christian centuries. Between the two communities there could be no "co-existence" in a state of indifference, as between two strangers. What set them against each other was, in fact, the very thing, the very person in whom their closest bond was forged, Jesus Christ. It was in the light of him that the Christians read and interpreted the sacred books inherited from the Jews, and were now to interpret Judaism.

It may be surprising, but it is unfortunately all too human, that in the course of the controversies and frictions of the ensuing years, both sides, to a great extent, so soon lost sight of what was still common to the two rival sisters, so as to emphasize only what separated and contrasted them, while on the Christian side even St Paul's essential views on the destiny of Israel were so often practically forgotten. During

[4] A Greek word meaning "dispersion": used for the Jewish communities outside Palestine.

those first four centuries which were the decisive period for the formation of the tradition and institutions of both Christianity and rabbinical Judaism, the need to define each by comparison with the other, to distinguish and differentiate each from the other in the eyes of the pagan population and the imperial authorities, left an indelible mark on the evolution of each one's thought. Doctrinal controversies and mutual grievances were fatally conducive to a hardening of the spiritual conflict and soon degraded it into a human conflict. The rapid evangelization of the pagan world tended to harden the attitude of Jewry, while the resistance of the Jewish communities irritated the Christians. The mass conversion of the pagans brought into the Church a certain heritage of anti-Jewish feelings and also a patrimony of Greco-Roman culture which had the fatal effect of making the Church appear to the Jews even more a "Church of the Gentiles". At the same time a last link between the two communities was severed, when the Jewish-Christian Church became isolated and finally disappeared. Then, too, the contrast between the legally privileged position of the Jews and the illegal, precarious and perilous situation of the Christians in the Empire was another source of friction and resentment.

With the accession and conversion of Constantine in 312, the political situation was completely reversed. Catholicism, but lately an illegal and persecuted religion, became practically the official religion of the Empire and found itself for a long time (except for a few short periods) associated with the power, first of the Empire, then of the Christian kingdoms and principalities of the Middle Ages. Through the same event, the privileged legal situation of Judaism was compromised and finally condemned. Gradually but rapidly there arose a conception of the Christian Empire and of civil and ecclesiastical legislation, according to which only Christians possessed full rights.[5] With paganism eliminated and heresies

[5] Later, Islam imposed a very similar position on both Jews and Christians, in the countries where its rule extended. But the relations between Islam and Israel do not form part of our subject-matter.

persecuted, only the Jews, the already "traditional" adversaries, survived permanently in the heart of the Christian world, and had to bear the consequences of this turn of events.

The imperial and conciliar legislation enacted from the fourth century onwards was at first inspired solely by thoughts of defence. It aimed at eliminating all Jewish influence from Christian society, at relegating the Jews to the "ban" of the Empire, at excluding them from the administrative and economic structure of society. The culmination of this development, though still distant, was the ghetto, and that isolation-centre of the Jews in the midst of the Christian people was an all too fertile seed-bed for all the ignorance, prejudices and myths which led to the wildest and most obstinate delusions and slanders.

The same motives, the same tendencies are found in the theological teaching about the Jews formulated—often with extreme rigour—by the preachers and ecclesiastical writers of this time, including the most illustrious. This legislation and teaching are largely explained by the fact that Jewish proselytism was still very active and the Jewish communities, cut off from discussion with the Christians, exerted a sort of fascination over the often uncouth and still imperfectly Christianized populations, by reason of their antiquity, knowledge of the Scriptures, culture, the beauty of their worship, etc. This fascination could not fail to appear dangerous to the authorities of Church and Empire. The hardened enmities and embittered controversies which were the rule, together, no doubt, with certain social ill-feeling, did the rest. The development thus begun, in teaching and legislation, never ceased to grow in the direction of hardness, contempt and enmity towards the Jews, profoundly impregnating the mind, the sensibility, the imagination, the language and all the traditions of medieval Christians. It was especially from the time of the First Crusade that this development produced its fruits of bloodshed, and it was then that the darkest ages of Jewish history began, from the twelfth century to the fifteenth.

Those ages of massacres, spoliations and oppression, of precarious and persecuted life, left an indelible mark on Jewish tradition, spirituality and feelings. The actual story was, of course, much more diverse and complex than this summary sketch suggests. But it was necessary at this point to recall, if only in a few words, that long past whose grievous heritage is still all too present, in the habits of thought, the feelings, the countless traditions of Christians and Jews alike, affecting even the structure of society, and those invisible psychological barriers which still survive, long after the institutional barriers have disappeared.

JEWS AND CHRISTIANS IN THE MODERN WORLD

In 1791, fifteen years after the same principle had been laid down in the Constitution of the United States of America, the Constituent Assembly of the French Revolution voted the emancipation of the Jews, gave them, that is, their full and equal rights as free citizens. This event is in a way the counterpart of that turning-point fifteen hundred years earlier, the coming of the Christian Empire. Within a few decades, all the countries of Europe had followed the movement thus begun.[6] This reintegration of the Jews into society in the countries of Christian tradition, and the process of assimilation to which it has given rise, have had incalculable effects on relations between the Jewish and Christian worlds. Normal relations between the two, which for centuries had been practically impossible, could now be resumed, even if the resumption has been slowed down by the after-effects of the past, often thwarted by political and economic circumstances, and too often made null and void by the decay of Christianity on one side and of real Judaism on the other. Nonetheless, little by little, links, exchanges, friendships have been formed, allowing Christians and Jews to see each other as they are,

[6] In England the Jews, expelled under Edward I, were readmitted under Oliver Cromwell in 1656, but political emancipation was not completed till 1858. (*Trans.*)

to become interested in each other, to ask questions about each other.

Until quite recently, all this did not hold back some Christian circles, still hampered by a "traditional" antisemitism, from alliances and collusions with the new forms of political, national and racialist antisemitism.[7] It needed the development and excesses of this last to force the Christian world to realize more clearly the real nature and malice of antisemitism.

This brutal demonstration was provided by Hitler's régime, with its openly pagan ideology, its monstrous and methodical savagery, which in a few years destroyed six million Jews, for the sole "crime" of being Jews. These incredible events have provoked an unprecedented reaction among many Christians, in Germany, in the occupied countries and throughout the world. Faced with such facts, no Christian worthy of the name can fail to question himself about the causes and implications of the tragedy, or to realize how grave and urgent is the problem of his own attitude, his responsibilities and his duties, with regard to the Jews. The pagan hatred which the persecutor showed for both Jews and Christians, the trials endured in common, the mutual aid and the friendships born in the crucible of suffering have given many Christians a better understanding of the solidarity which binds them to the people of the Old Covenant. These experiences have left such a mark on a whole Christian élite that since the war, with many attempts at reflection and examination of conscience, various enterprises are constantly developing in the Christian world of today and are already more widely affecting the rising generation.

The birth of the State of Israel in 1948 was another powerful factor which made the fact of Jewry a matter of the most urgent importance for the attention and consideration of the

[7] The word dates from the nineteenth century, though the thing it denotes is ancient. The term is neither logical nor exact, in the past or the present, but it has become so common that it can be used not inaccurately, and it is even difficult to do without it.

Christian world. This creation of a Jewish State, as striking and novel of its kind as the catastrophe which a few years earlier had brutally destroyed a great part of the Jewish world, bore the aspect of an astonishing human achievement, the mere knowledge of which was enough to destroy many prejudices. But it also bore the signs of a providential event, strangely linked with the facts of the Bible, and inviting the Christian to view the political fact afresh, in a religious perspective.

Yet all these facts of contemporary history would not suffice to explain the present evolution of the relations between the Christian world and the Jewish. The way for this had been prepared for more than half a century by unseen currents which, after the interruption of the war, were able to burst forth abruptly and more widely, on the level of the Church's life. Here the biblical revival has played an extremely important part. In a Christian life taught and lived in its biblical perspectives, Israel recovers its true place; the patrimony of the Bible, common to Israel and the Church, recovers all its value, and the bond between Israel and the Church all its reality. So many sincere Christians of former generations were, as to the "Jewish question", at the mercy of ideological and political influences really incompatible with the plain implications of their faith, and this was simply because Israel could find no place in their too abstract and narrow Christian outlook. In this respect, the present development, with its repercussions in the field of the catechism, preaching, pastoral work, the action of the liturgy, etc., is radically transforming the conditions of our attitude towards Judaism.

At the same time (largely owing to a more acute awareness of the biblical, historical and ecclesiological dimensions of Christianity), aspirations and efforts towards unity have come to the fore in the modern Christian world. Now the question of relations between separated Christians has obvious analogies with that of the relations between Christians and Jews. In both cases, the problem is (among others) how to transcend the narrowness of an individualist point of view and face the problem on the plane of the Church. We have to rise above grievances and polemics, which can only embitter, in order to seek a *rapprochement* and a fraternal dialogue, based on mutual respect, and to explore more fully our common heritage. We have to detect and honestly oppose (in ourselves first of all) those factors of separation and misunderstanding which history and human frailty have superimposed on the original doctrinal differences. Because of these analogies, we can already note without surprise that any progress in one of these fields—inter-Church relations or Jewish-Christian relations—has rapid repercussions in the other.

Under the combined influence of these different factors, many attempts are being made in the Christian world to recover and deepen Christian understanding of Israel's destiny, to define and propagate a genuinely Christian attitude to Judaism and the Jews, especially in all forms of religious teaching, and also to combat whatever is opposed to this development: the leaven of contempt and hatred, inveterate prejudices backed up by the irrational forces of passions, habit, ignorance and inertia. The obstacles are considerable. An immense layer of dust, accumulated over fifteen centuries, is not cleared in a few years. But signs of progress increase daily, while in the Jewish world, now emerging from its centuries of isolation and its defensive position as an oppressed minority, there are many signs to prove the existence of parallel trends, favourable to the development of contacts, *rapprochements*, discussions and collaboration. In the Church, the hierarchy is beginning to lend these efforts its increasing support and backing. Following his predecessors (and especially Pius XI, whose firm stand against the Nazi ideology before the second World War impressed Catholic and Jewish opinion alike), the present Pope, John XXIII, has been eager since his accession to show his interest in the Church's attitude to the Jews. Among other things, he has suppressed three passages in the Church's prayer which might mislead the faithful and did offend the Jews.[8] Similarly, in our time, in 1960, no doubt for the first time in the history of the Church (at least in this spirit), a bishop—Cardinal Liénart—devoted his Lenten Pastoral to "The Christian Conscience and the Jewish Question".

Such signs, increasing in number, reveal something both new and important. For nineteen centuries the gulf between the Church and Israel continued to grow deeper, the conflict to harden, its real significance to be concealed. But today, just as between separated Christians, the attitude of age-long estrangement is beginning to give way, still cautiously but clearly, to one of mutual approach. The historical and religious importance of this fact is considerable. It involves tasks and responsibilities which no Christian of our day can decline. That is why it seemed impossible to present the Christian public of our day with a brief introduction to Judaism and the knowledge of our "elder brethren in the faith" without first insisting rather strongly on the climate in which any such approach must now be made.

[8] These were the notorious expressions *perfidia judaica* and *perfidi judaei* in the prayer for the Jews in the liturgy of Good Friday (where already Pius XII had restored the genuflection, the omission of which, for this prayer alone, had an offensive nature); a passage in the Act of Consecration of the human race to the Sacred Heart (when introduced in 1925 by Pius XI it was considered by all a happy innovation, which just shows the speed of the present development); a passage in the Ritual for the Baptism of Adults. The two latter equally concerned Moslems and even pagans.

CHAPTER II

A GLANCE AT THE HISTORY OF ISRAEL

ANCIENT JUDAISM

It is obviously impossible in a few pages to give a sketch of the whole history of Judaism. All that is offered here are some sign-posts, indispensable if the main stages in the formation of Judaism, with its traditions and institutions, are to be assigned to their place in history. Without some knowledge of these stages it would be impossible to grasp the essential features of the character of Judaism. On the supposition that the reader has some knowledge of the history of Israel in biblical times, this sketch is confined to the formation of Judaism in the post-biblical era, though certain features of the biblical history which may illuminate later developments are recalled.

In the ancient history of God's people there is a period which prefigures what was to be its condition after the destruction of Jerusalem and its Temple in A.D. 70, and the disappearance of its political and national centre in Palestine. This is the Babylonian Exile of the sixth century B.C. This exile of the flower of the kingdom of Juda proved a kind of providential apprenticeship for Israel's later existence. It was during the Exile and the ensuing Restoration that there was formed, under the influence of the last great prophets and the first great *sopherim* or "scribes", what came to be the foundation of Israel's unity, strength and survival, the *Torah*,[1] gift of the Covenant, charter of the religious and national (i.e. theocratic) life of the people of God. The same period saw the planning of the internal structure which enabled Israel to survive and to safeguard its cohesion and its heritage when it was dispersed. The life of the exiles was organized, in practice, on the framework of the community rather than of the nation. After the return, the restored nation was thought of as a community, an assembly of God. To this development correspond the beginnings of the synagogue, the place of meeting, prayer, study and teaching, an essentially local institution, capable of infinite multiplication, corresponding to the structure of the community, the foundation of the community's autonomy and spiritual vitality. It is true that after the restoration under Cyrus Israel recovered for some centuries its national centre and its centralized sacrificial worship in the Temple. But during this period the communities of an ever-increasing Dispersion existed or were being formed. The Jews, deportees or captives, voluntary recruits in various armies, emigrants fleeing the insecurity of the Promised Land (long the thoroughfare and battlefield of the great empires), or simply overflowing that poor and narrow land by their numbers and vitality, never ceased to scatter after the Exile, during the Persian period, and still more during the times of unification and internationalization of the Mediterranean world which marked the Greek period and the rule of Rome.

Though spiritually they looked towards Jerusalem and the Promised Land, the communities of the Diaspora enjoyed great autonomy. This gave them a certain flexibility in adapting themselves to life among other peoples and civilizations. Without any institutional connecting link, they maintained very close contacts both with one another and with the centre in Palestine. They were thus able to preserve strong mutual cohesion, while still proving themselves very open, on the whole, to exchanges with their surroundings.

[1] *Torah* here means primarily the Pentateuch.

But the real starting-point of the post-biblical evolution is to be found in the period of the birth of Christianity. What is the general picture of Judaism at this time?

The Jews then represented from ten to fifteen per cent. of the population of the Empire, a total of between five and eight million persons, of whom more than three-quarters lived in the communities of the Diaspora and less than a quarter in Palestine. This division roughly corresponds to two groups with different characteristics. On the one hand there was the Judaism of Palestine and Syria, with part of the Babylonian Diaspora, which kept its Semitic language and culture and offered some resistance, not unanimous but serious, to Hellenization and foreign influences. On the other hand, we find Hellenized Judaism, comprising the majority of the communities of the Diaspora, which had adopted the language of the Hellenistic world and, as far as was compatible with their faith, its civilization, even to the point of translating and reading the Scriptures themselves in Greek, especially in the version called "of the Seventy" (the Septuagint). This was a Judaism which was open-minded, humanist, "liberal" in a certain sense (which is not the modern sense), ready to adapt itself to the world about it, inclined to universalize its religion, to spiritualize its worship (the Temple and the sacrifices), to interpret the Scriptures allegorically rather than literally. This Hellenistic Judaism, with its chief intellectual centre at Alexandria, was at its zenith at the very moment when Christianity was born. In the pagan world around it, it exercised a considerable influence and carried on an active and fruitful proselytism. The greatest and most celebrated representative of this Judaism was Philo of Alexandria, a philosopher, theologian and exegete. But of all the considerable literature to which this Hellenistic Judaism gave birth only a small part has been preserved.

It is an astounding fact that in the history of post-biblical Judaism we can find scarcely any further traces of this powerful and flourishing branch of ancient Judaism. From the second Christian century its image begins to fade and then rapidly disappears, largely absorbed into the expanding Christian communities, for which it had providentially prepared the way, or else recaptured by those of a new Jewish Diaspora of the Palestinian type. Its last manifestations, along with many elements of its special heritage, have been preserved in the Christian tradition—for example in the Christian literature of Alexandria—more than in the Jewish. Post-biblical Judaism was to develop entirely out of Palestinian Judaism.

Palestinian Judaism, however, was itself far from uniform. The apocryphal books, contemporary historians, traces preserved in traditional Jewish literature, recently discovered documents, as well as the New Testament, give us a glimpse of a mass of "trends" and "sects", such as the apocalyptic circles, the groups of baptists, ascetics or dissidents, like the sect of the New Covenant of Damascus, the Essenes or the members of the Qumrân community. Two important groups, however, were rivals for supreme influence, the Sadducees and the Pharisees.

The former corresponded in the main to a priestly and political aristocracy. After the Restoration, the religious leadership of Judaism was still in the hands of the priestly class. But after Alexander the Great's conquest, this class yielded to Hellenization and deviated from the pure tradition of Judaism. With the Hasmonean kings, it succeeded to the temporal power and turned to political preoccupations and ambitions. In the period which concerns us, we see it ready to compromise with the foreign power and at the same time shutting itself up in a rigid political and religious conservatism, holding strictly to the letter of the Torah and rejecting the living tradition. Though their political influence was great, the Sadducees had but little authority over the religious life of the people, and it was only in secondary or heterodox trends of later Judaism that some traces of their characteristic position were preserved.

Spiritual authority passed almost entirely into the hands of the Pharisees. Though they claimed to be the successors of the priestly scribes of the Restoration, these lay teachers, these "pious" (*Chasidim*), these "separated" (*perushim*, whence the name Pharisees),[2] only appeared as a recognized and influential group in the second century B.C. Sprung from the people, full of zeal for the study and observance of the Torah, they were the defenders and interpreters of the living tradition, of an *oral Torah* alongside the *written Torah*, enabling the latter to be constantly adapted to new circumstances and concrete needs. It was they, with their evolutionary concept of the Torah and its interpretation, who elaborated more precisely and explicitly most of the doctrines of later Judaism, doctrines which were equally adopted, to a great extent, in Christian tradition. It was they who bequeathed to rabbinical Judaism[3] its characteristic structure: a religion centred on the Torah, developed and supplemented by the oral Law, which is claimed to be an interpretation (*midrash*) and is expressed either in authoritative decisions (*halakhah*) or in teaching by parables, etc. (*haggadah*). Eminent among the Pharisaic doctors are certain great figures, such as the illustrious founders of schools, the rigorous Shammai and the gentle, humane Hillel, whose influence eventually prevailed in the development of Judaism.

Parallel with the formation of the Pharisaic tradition, the synagogue liturgy took shape, centred on the reading of the Scriptures (the Torah and the Prophets), according to a cycle of lessons which was gradually fixed. The reading was amplified, commented on and explained in Aramaic—the language commonly spoken in Palestine at this time—in the form of popular homilies, and we find their themes and echoes in

[2] Considering that St Paul still proudly claimed to be a Pharisee (Phil. 3. 5), it is a curious fact that the habit of reading the Gospels in the light of later conflicts has given the name "Pharisee", in Christian tradition, an offensive sense which is not historically justified.

[3] The rabbis were precisely the successors of the Pharisaic doctors (*Rabbi*, "my master"). The rabbi is still a man of study, teaching, preaching and law: his function is neither priestly nor liturgical nor pastoral, though in modern Judaism his position often tends to resemble that of a pastor.

the surviving *Palestinian Targums* (Aramaic paraphrases of the Pentateuch, the Prophets and the five "Scrolls") and in the Midrash literature. While the substance of this tradition of reading and teaching passed into later tradition, its forms of expression were largely supplanted in rabbinical Judaism by the tradition formed some centuries later in the Babylonian Jewish schools.

RABBINICAL JUDAISM

Pharisaic Judaism, that vigorous and representative branch of first-century Judaism, was itself in danger of being swallowed up in the catastrophe which befell Palestinian Judaism in the year 70, with the fall of Jerusalem, culminating in the crushing of Bar Kokhba's revolt in 130. It was saved through the survival, continuity and revival of the rabbinical schools. During the actual siege of Jerusalem, Yohanan ben Zakkai, one of the heads of the "house" of Hillel, left the city and obtained authorization from Vespasian to open a school at Yabne, in Galilee, thus building a bridge between the two great periods of Jewish history. The opening of this school was followed by others, notably at Sephoris and Tiberias. A new Assembly or Sanhedrin was reconstituted, now without political power, but called to exercise an undisputed religious and judicial authority. To its president Rome accorded the title of *nasi* or patriarch. The Sadducean priesthood having disappeared together with the Temple, the Pharisees, and especially the disciples of Hillel, were henceforth masters of the Sanhedrin and, to a great extent, of the future destinies of Judaism. The intense religious activity, of which Yabne was the first centre, was maintained for several centuries, but in the fourth century the great Palestinian schools began to decline when, after the triumph of Christianity, the position of the Jews in Palestine changed for the worse. This decline was consummated when the emperor Theodosius II suppressed the "patriarchate" in 425.

But meanwhile, beginning in the second century and still

more in the third, some doctors trained in Palestine, who had joined the flourishing Jewish communities in Babylonia, laid there the foundations of new schools or rabbinical academies, notably those of Sura, Nehardea and Pumbedita, which soon became very prosperous. At first they were active alongside the Palestinian schools, but on the decline of the latter they took up the torch of tradition and prolonged the golden age of the talmudic tradition for a full century longer. Towards the end of the fifth century it was the turn of the Babylonian communities and schools to be persecuted, and they were obliged to keep their activities in the shade. But the Moslem conquest soon transformed conditions of life for the Jewish communities in the Middle East. Favoured by the tolerant policy of the Arabs during the early centuries after the conquest, the Babylonian "exilarchate" was revived, and the authority of the *Gaonim*, the Babylonian heads of schools, was extended over the whole Diaspora, though it met with opposition from some heterodox sects and trends, even in Babylonia. In the tenth century the attitude of the Arabs changed and the rabbinical academies, along with the Jewish communities, suffered from it. But in this period the schools of Cairo, Kairwan, Cordoba, Narbonne, etc., were already growing up in the West, and these were to take over the heritage of the older schools and ensure the continuity of the tradition.

On the whole, the important Jewish communities in the lands conquered by Islam experienced tolerable conditions in the Middle Ages, though with ups and downs, but they suffered from isolation and finally a certain stagnation. They ended by preserving their patrimony, their own traditions of language (especially the Jewish-Arabic) and of rite, in many cases till our days, but they did not play an important part in the evolution of Judaism as a whole.

It was otherwise with the two great centres of Jewish life which began to be formed in Europe at the very time when the great eastern centres of Judaism were declining.

The most extraordinary epic was that of Spanish Jewry,

which enjoyed a truly golden age under Moorish rule, from the ninth to the thirteenth century and, in spite of vicissitudes caused by the Christian reconquest, preserved its heritage until the great final expulsion of 1492. The importance of the social, political, economic, intellectual, scientific and artistic positions of Spanish Jewry at the peak of its prosperity is without parallel in history, as is the *modus vivendi* it established with the surrounding populations. Traces are still clearly perceptible of the important part it played in the formation of the whole culture of Spain, and also, by its rôle of intermediary between the Arab and Christian civilizations, in the formation of all European culture. The number of its strictly Jewish books (though they were generally written in Arabic), theological and philosophical as well as poetical and mystical, is likewise impressive. Thus there grew up in Spain a type of Jewish life, *Sephardi* Judaism, having its own liturgical rite, its own vernacular (*Ladino* or Spanish-Jewish), its own style of Jewish humanism, a whole inheritance. The Sephardi communities, settled after the expulsion of 1492 in the Levantine lands and North Africa, but also in the Netherlands, England and France, preserve this heritage to this day.

Spanish Jewry has provided Judaism with some of its greatest thinkers, including the most illustrious of all, Moses ben Maimon, or Maimonides, in the twelfth century, who is to Judaism what Albert the Great and Thomas Aquinas (who quotes him, moreover) are to the Church. But the theological and philosophical works of the great Spanish-Jewish thinkers have remained, for the most part, on the fringe of the development of Jewish life and tradition. It was on either bank of the Rhine, rather than in Spain, that the rabbinical studies which were to leave their mark on Jewish tradition prospered at this time and produced works of lasting influence, such as the commentary on the Pentateuch and the glosses on the Talmud of Babylonia, composed by Rashi (Rabbi Solomon ben Isaac), the famous teacher of Troyes in the eleventh century.

Here we encounter the other great home of Jewish life in

Europe, centred at first on the Rhineland, with Germany and the east of France, then, from the end of the Middle Ages, on central and eastern Europe, and especially Poland. This is *Ashkenazi* (i.e. German) Judaism, which had, too, its own rite, its vernacular tongue (*Yiddish* or German-Jewish), its characteristic style of life and its own culture, much more exclusively Jewish, religious and rabbinical than that of Sephardi Judaism. It too has shown extraordinary vitality and powers of resistance and preservation, which enabled it to grow in numbers, to maintain strong cohesion and to put forth intense activity in study and religious life, under the hardest conditions. It was in the heart of Ashkenazi Judaism that rabbinical studies reached their highest development, at least in their extent and their central rôle in the community life, if not in the scope of the works they produced. It is due above all to the talmudic schools of Ashkenazi Judaism that rabbinical tradition has survived to our time.

To appreciate the importance in Jewish history of these rabbinical institutions, whereby tradition was handed on, constantly explored and applied to life, we must remember that Judaism possesses no supreme teaching body, no hierarchy, no unitary organization. The unity of its faith, tradition and religious "practice" has been preserved essentially by the universally accepted authority of the authentic representatives of tradition: the great rabbinical academies of the first millennium, which were at once schools, legislative organs and tribunals; the great rabbinical conferences of the Middle Ages; the personal authority of certain great doctors, of their successors or disciples. But the living nature of these authorities and their essentially oral teaching, so far from making the written formulation and codification of tradition superfluous, actually demanded it. The undisputed authority of the great written sources of rabbinical tradition came to serve as both the criterion and the foundation for the authority of the oral teaching. So now, having sketched the historical outline of the development of rabbinical tradition, we must rapidly describe its principal formularies.

THE RABBINICAL SOURCES[4]

Before embarking on the sources, it may be well to emphasize that *the* essential source of Jewish tradition is always the Book of books, the Bible, and in the Bible particularly the Pentateuch, the Torah. From the birth of Judaism in the strict sense, at the return from the Exile, tradition began to assume an interpretative character, attaching itself constantly to the letter of the Book. In this sense, everything in Jewish tradition is *midrash*, search, search for the meaning, the deep meaning, the ever-present meaning of Scripture. The definitive compilation of the Torah and the body of inspired books, the fixing of the Canon of the Scriptures and the transmission of the sacred text—the work of the *Massoretes*—had already supplied precisely the same need as that which inspired the formation of all the rabbinical literature: the need to fix, preserve and transmit tradition, and at the same time to make it actual and present. Thus, after the written Law, there came to be fixed in writing the *oral Law*, that is, the authentic, living teaching which is ascribed, like the other, to Moses, and in its essential elements has the same authority as the written Law.

The vital period in the fixing of the oral Law was during the first two Christian centuries, at the time when, in the schools of the Yabne region, the *tannaim* ("repeaters": teachers who handed on tradition by repeating it, teaching it orally) were elaborating, expounding, interpreting, illustrating and untiringly applying the Torah of Moses. The close of this period was dominated by the unrivalled authority of Rabbi Judah ha-Nasi, or Judah the Saint. It was he who completed the work begun by his predecessors, especially Akiba and Meir, by elaborating, in six "orders", a real "Summa" of the works of generations of *tannaim*: the *Mishnah* (repetition). Chiefly moral, juridical and practical in

[4] Here we deal only with rabbinical tradition properly so-called, of a "canonical" character. Some important traditional documents connected with Jewish mystical trends are considered in Chapter VI.

character (always in the sense of essentially religious "practice" and "legislation"), the Mishnah was at once accepted as the "canonical" collection above all others, the authentic and authoritative expression of the oral Law. It impressed its character on all rabbinical literature and became the base of the two Talmuds and of all rabbinical jurisprudence. Similar contemporary traditions which did not find a place in the Mishnah were in their turn assembled in supplementary collections, called *Tosephtah* and *Baraitot*.

In the same period a beginning was made with the formation of exegetic collections which are not systematic treatises, but constitute a kind of connected, very free, commentaries on different books of the Bible, and are called, in a more technical sense, *midrashim* (researches). The oldest of these *midrashim*—collections of which were still being formed well into the Middle Ages—are called *tannaitic,* for they continue a tradition going back, like the Mishnah, to the doctors of the first two centuries of our era. Like the Mishnah, they are of a mainly *halachic* tendency (from *halachah*, walk, step, path, in the sense of law, precept), that is, they are legal and practical.

From the third to the fifth century, in the schools of Palestine and Babylonia, generations of rabbis called *amoraim* devoted themselves to discussing, annotating and explaining the Mishnah, comparing it with other sources of tradition, enriching it with new applications, illustrating it with the traditions of the *haggadic* Midrash and all the resources of knowledge, biblical, rabbinical and even secular. These developments and discussions were later incorporated in the *Gemarah*, which, together with the Mishnah, whose order and arrangement it follows, constitutes the *Talmud* ("teaching"), or rather the two Talmuds. There is the Talmud of Jerusalem, or *Yerushalmi*, elaborated in the schools of Palestine, which is much the shorter, more suggestive but also more obscure, sometimes containing older elements of tradition, and there is also the Talmud of Babylonia, or *Babli,* completed a century later, fuller and more meticulous, with a closer and more subtle dialectic. As the Babylonian schools survived the Palestinian by several centuries, it was mainly their tradition which prevailed in later Judaism. Thus it was the Babylonian Talmud which was far more used and studied and became the principal repertory of tradition, the foundation of all rabbinical knowledge and teaching. Besides, it effectively contains a great part of the traditions, both ancient and more recent, which are found in other rabbinical sources. It is a universe, a sort of encyclopedia of rabbinical knowledge, but without any methodical plan, since for the most part it reports, with great freedom of style, the teachings and scholastic discussions of generations of masters. It thus constitutes both a depositary and a starting-point for new discussions and developments. Jewish traditional teaching (especially in Ashkenazi Judaism) mainly consists to this day in teaching the pupil to understand and use the Talmud and instructing him how to derive rules of action and decision, a way of life and holiness, from the involved discussions of the doctors.

But the increasing complication of this tradition of the schools called for more systematic codification to make it easier to consult and use the sources. For this reason, in the twelfth century, Maimonides, the "Eagle of the Synagogue", undertook the task of clearing up and recapitulation, in order to clarify the doctrine of the Talmud. His *Mishneh Torah* ("Repetition of the Law") is a methodical exposition of rabbinical legislation and jurisprudence. This innovation, at first opposed, was then welcomed and much utilized. The latest of these great codifications, the *Shulchan Aruch* ("Prepared Table"), the work of Joseph Caro at Safed in Galilee, in the sixteenth century, is also the most classical and remains the standard of Jewish orthodoxy to this day.

The largely, though not exclusively, legal character of this literature, as represented in the summary indications we have given, might easily mislead the reader who is not familiar with Judaism. To grasp the real place of this literature in Jewish life, we must first remember that much of the legislation and jurisprudence contained in it applied to the civil life of the nation or community; we must remember, too, the fundamentally religious value and the all-embracing nature of the Law in Jewish life, which knows no distinction between sacred and profane; finally, and above all, that the talmudic literature, of capital importance though it is, does not constitute the sole source of the religious life of Judaism. Beside it and above it there are the Scriptures; the Torah, the Prophets, the Writings, especially the Psalms, with which the Jewish soul is constantly penetrated and nourished. There is prayer and the Synagogue worship, a no less essential food of the Jew's religious life. Finally, besides the rabbinical writings, there is in the Jewish tradition a mystical element which has been strong enough to penetrate rabbinical literature itself in many places, and continues to hold a prominent place in Judaism. For the sake of clarity, we shall deal with these different sources of Jewish life in separate chapters, but obviously such sharp distinctions are not wholly appropriate.

After these considerations on the sources of Jewish tradition, the reader might perhaps expect some observations on the theology of Judaism. And it is true that the encounter with Moslem theological thought and the discovery, through the medium of the Arabs, of Greek philosophy—later followed by the encounter with Christian theology—gave rise, in the ninth century, to Judaism's first attempts at theological elaboration. From the tenth century onwards, we find a whole series of important thinkers, philosophers and theologians, who were often poets at the same time. There were Saadia, Solomon ibn Gabirol, Judah Halevi, Moses Maimonides, etc., who enriched Jewish thought and literature with major works of lasting value. But this theological enterprise, like all attempts at conceptual systematization of the content of Israel's tradition, was doomed to remain on the fringe of the main stream of the life of Judaism. In that life theology has never held the organic position it holds in the Church or in Islam. As we shall see more precisely in the doctrinal exposition in Chapter IV, this results from the very nature of

Judaism, whose faith and religion are inseparable from a concrete history and a Law to be carried out and, because of this twofold fact, are less capable of formulation in abstract categories than in any other religion. The study of the Jewish theologians is not without interest, but it is not indispensable for a knowledge or understanding of the tradition and life of Judaism.

CHAPTER III

JUDAISM TODAY

Isolated in the ghetto, practically cut off from outside influence, Judaism was able at leisure to preserve and shape its soul, its tradition, its way of life, its unity, all based essentially on its faith, its fidelity to the Torah. Emancipation brought about an abrupt and radical change in this state of affairs, which through countless vicissitudes had remained for centuries strangely static. At the same time, the upheavals accompanying the spread from west to east of both emancipation and the birth of the modern world gave rise to a large-scale migration, which in successive waves uprooted millions of Jews from eastern Europe to central and western Europe and to America, quickly transforming the whole aspect of the Jewish world. In consequence of these changes most communities of the medieval type were progressively dislocated, traditional standards were broken down and many Jews were suddenly confronted with the modern world and its problems, as they encountered the civilization of their new neighbours. Finally, there was an increasing assimilation to these new neighbours, especially where these proved really welcoming. The other side of this process, with the gradual abandonment of the ancestral way of life, was a weakening of the traditional ties and authorities. For the first time in two thousand years, the fundamental continuity and unity of Judaism were in danger of being compromised. Just when a large part of the Jewish world, in consequence of emancipation, was able to display great social and intellectual vitality, its new associations and worldly interests made it less Jewish, and threatened, little by little, to dissolve these important groups of Jews. It is true that besides the religious forces, which after all were still powerful, there existed a cohesive influence, less definite but not less real (even where tradition was largely relaxed), which often strove to define and organize itself on purely cultural, social or Jewish national bases, as in the case of the Zionist movement. In spite of these influences and efforts, there can be no doubt that assimilated western Jewry would have been even more rapidly despoiled of its Jewish values if the constant arrival of new waves of immigrants from the East had not continually brought in fresh reserves of Jewish tradition. But while these reinforcements could check and partly counterbalance the consequences of assimilation, they could not arrest this irreversible process.

Traditional Jewish life was in fact strictly bound up with the homogeneous circle of the community, where all was centred on the performance of the Torah. When the Jews, as individuals, as families or as groups, were planted down in the non-Jewish surroundings of the modern world, a new and difficult problem arose, inevitably starting new spiritual trends and new religious choices.

These new movements had begun, even before the legal emancipation of the Jews, with the very first steps of their social and cultural emancipation, in Germany, in the age of the "Enlightenment", in the circle of Moses Mendelssohn. It is there that we must look for the origin of the most radical answer to the new problem confronting Judaism, the answer of the "Reform", or Reformed Judaism, also called, in different countries and periods, Liberal or Progressive Judaism. It was a tendency, a type of Judaism, rather than any precise and uniform doctrine. The religious liberalism of the latter half of the eighteenth century and the first half of the nineteenth provided this movement with some of its fundamental ideas: progressive revelation, a religion without dogmas and subject to the criteria of reason, the predominance of moralism, a liberal humanism hostile to all particularism.[1] But above and beyond these ideas there was, and there certainly still is, increasingly, a living Jewish faith which seeks a form of expression adapted to the modern world. The aim of the "Liberals" of this school is to readapt the worship and institutions of Judaism in order to safeguard the authentic substance of the biblical, prophetic and mystical heritage of Israel, to restore them to esteem, to make them universally accessible. Born in Germany, this Liberal Judaism then spread abroad, especially in the Anglo-Saxon countries. Very radical and sometimes very negative in its beginnings, it has excited violent reactions and bitter controversy. At present, especially since the events which have again upset the balance of the Jewish world, the opposition between the Reform and the defenders of tradition is beginning to slacken. Little by little, much of traditional Judaism is accepting inevitable adaptations, while the Liberals, for their part, are gradually abandoning reforms which are clearly incompatible with the essence of Judaism, and trying rather to restore contact with tradition.

Confronted with the Reform, Orthodox Judaism has been able, on the whole, to preserve the traditional teaching and observances untouched, with some stiffening of its positions, indeed, where it felt itself menaced by the innovators. In spite of considerable losses, it still holds a very strong position in the Jewish world.

But there are other defenders of tradition who have tried to open a middle way between integral orthodoxy and the liberal reform, and to reconcile traditional practice and doctrine with modern conditions of life and forms of thought. This neo-orthodoxy is at the root of conservative or traditional Judaism, which holds a very important place in the centre of the present world-view of Judaism, while including in itself diverse tendencies and shades of thought.

Each of these three main divisions of modern religious Judaism possesses its own institutions, its Rabbinate, its

[1] Particularism: the tendency to limit God's saving purpose to Israel in particular.

synagogues, its schools—both rabbinical seminaries or universities of the modern type or talmudic schools (*Yeshivot*) of the traditional type—its different associations and organizations. But there also exist many groups for cultural, social or charitable action, in which Jews belonging to contrasted schools of thought collaborate without difficulty.

Later in this chapter will be found a brief sketch of modern Judaism, in which is indicated the respective importance of these three main organized forms of modern Jewish religious life. But a great many Jews remain outside the organized communities belonging to any of these three tendencies.

In spite of these persistent divisions, and its lack of unity of doctrine or organization, Judaism has recovered a stronger internal cohesion in our time and a certain unity in its aspirations. This evolution is due to two great facts, some of the consequences of which have been already mentioned in the first chapter: first, the Nazi massacres, then the birth of the State of Israel. These two great events put an end to the evolution which had been going on for a century and abruptly altered the balance of the Jewish world. And different as the two events were, they combined in their effect on the Jewish world as a whole. Each, in fact, provoked a sort of reawakening by sharply recalling a unique destiny, the consciousness of which had been somewhat deadened by a century of assimilation; each reinforced the feeling of solidarity between all Jews, and also the feeling of unity, indefinable but very real, since, with very few exceptions, Jews of the most divergent tendencies were seen to react in the same way to the destruction of European Judaism and to the Israeli resurgence.

Each of the two events tended to compel modern Jewry to reconsider its position and its future. On the one hand, the brutal destruction of the main homes of traditional Ashkenazi Judaism, by depriving western Jewry of a contribution and support which had hitherto been of vital importance, forced it to realize that it must now find its means of survival from within its own resources. This is especially true of American

Jewry, now conscious of the leadership which has devolved upon it, because of its numerical and economic strength, and of the responsibilities it must now shoulder in the destinies of all Jewry. On the other hand, the creation of a Jewish State, Israel—theoretically difficult to fit in to the outlook of traditional Judaism, which expected a return to the Holy Land only by a divine intervention in Messianic days—confronted the Jewish world with the question of the meaning and purpose of a dispersed Judaism (other than religious), now that the national element in Judaism has found its concrete expression in the new Israeli nation. And so, at the present juncture, the problem of the division of Judaism into several religious tendencies is to a certain extent passed over and relegated to a secondary place by the new problems—the new balance in the Jewish world, the relations between the State of Israel and the Diaspora, the meaning of the latter, with its orientation and future; finally, and perhaps the most important, above and beyond present divisions, a revival of religious Judaism for the generations to come, in both Israel and the Diaspora.

Such are the great problems confronting modern Jewry. But what is the concrete aspect, today, of the Jewish world?

First of all, some figures. Before the Second World War there were more than sixteen million Jews in the world, of whom about two-thirds (nine million) lived in Europe and about a third in America. Between 1938 and 1945 six million Jews perished in Europe. Today there remain about three and a half million in Europe, more than two million of whom are in Soviet Russia, cut off from the rest of the Jewish world and subject to a policy of assimilation which aims, no doubt, at their complete absorption. With about half a million Jews in Great Britain, there remain scarcely a million on the continent of Europe outside Russia, with only one stable and important group, more than 300,000, in France. Numerically, by far the most considerable group of Jews in the world is that of the United States, with more than five million members. If to them we add the Jewish communities of Canada and Latin America, we find that the American continent now harbours more than half the Jewish population of the world. Asia, apart from Israel, contains no important Jewish communities, nor does the African continent, apart from North Africa, whose ancient and still important Jewish populations are not now increasing.

Besides the preponderance now assumed by American Jewry, the great new factor is obviously Israel. Whereas before the last war the number of Zionist colonists was still less than half a million, the Jewish population of the new State is now rapidly approaching two millions. But even more significant than figures is the extraordinary concentration of Jewish values brought into Israel by immigrants coming from all quarters, and their regrouping in a predominantly Jewish society. This means that from now on, even before the different traditions have had time to take root and be organically harmonized, Israel is a home of Jewish life, culture and thought, whose influence is already being felt throughout the Jewish world.

Thus, while twenty years ago the principal home of Jewish life was in Europe, today Jewry possesses two centres, whose respective rôles are of course very different, Israel and the United States. The second fairly represents the modern Diaspora, a Judaism which, on the whole, has opted decisively for national assimilation, while desiring to safeguard or revive its own religious and cultural heritage and to play its part in the destinies of Judaism. Relations between the two great centres are very close, but are subject to some frictions, owing to the great differences in their respective situations and the difficulty they often experience in understanding each other's point of view. They are further complicated by the vital material aid which American Jewry has supplied and is still supplying to the State of Israel.

The positions occupied by the three great religious groups in these different parts of the world are very unequal. In Israel only Orthodox Judaism has a legal and organized existence, though all the other trends are found there. Things are roughly the same in the three countries of North Africa. In the United States the three forms of Judaism are about equal in numbers. In England, Jews are divided between Orthodox and Reform Judaism, in the proportion of about three to one.

What is common to all these Jewish communities, in such different situations and of such different trends, is the feeling that they are in a period of transition, at a turning-point of Jewish history; the feeling that the survival and renewal of religious Judaism can only be assured in so far as those in the rising generations who remain faithful to tradition succeed in becoming integrated to the modern world, and the others renew organic relations with the permanent values of Jewish tradition.

CHAPTER IV

THE MAIN LINES OF JEWISH DOCTRINE

GENERAL REMARKS

In our previous chapters we have attempted to "place" Judaism, in the life of the Jewish people, in the stages of its history and in its present state. Our next task is to study the Jewish religion itself, the nature and content of its faith, its fundamental teaching. But as this content is intimately bound up with the historical and actual relations of the people of Israel with God, it is difficult to separate what is "doctrine" in the Jewish tradition from what is "practice", that is, worship or morals. Israel's faith is a faithfulness to a divine choice, to a Covenant, to a Law, and an obedience to the call and commandments of God, before it is a belief implying a dogmatic content. As soon as an attempt is made to confine the essential content of Judaism within the framework of a systematic exposition of doctrines or dogmas, the danger of distorting its proper aspect arises. It is true that the great Jewish thinkers of the Middle Ages, like many modern authors, often tried to formulate the Credo of Judaism—Maimonides, for example, in his now classical "Thirteen Principles of faith"—and to construct a Jewish theology, on the model of the categories of Moslem or Christian theology, but all have to admit in the end that real, historic Judaism refuses to be confined in these categories. In order, then, to grasp the real nature of Judaism, we prefer to make a survey of it, passing in review the great fundamental themes, the vital structures of its teaching, practices and prayer. From these observations as a whole, rather than from any artificial synthesis, it is hoped that there will emerge a picture of Judaism, summary but faithful, alive and comprehensive, and all these observations are confined to essentials. In general, there will be no reference to historical evolution, to sources, to minor diversities, or to learned theological treatises. Only the main, constant factors of Judaism, its permanent and present features are to be found here.

THE GOD OF ISRAEL

The title of this section must not be supposed to suggest that Judaism's idea of God is in any way limited or particularist. In the course of biblical history, thanks to the work of the prophets, the Hebrews had outgrown this sort of limitation and come to the knowledge of a Creator God, God of the world and of history, God of the nations as well as of the chosen people. What this title means to express is the concrete and historical character of Israel's faith: the God of Jewish faith is the God who has spoken to Israel, chosen Israel, established a special relationship between Israel and himself, made himself known to Israel in order to make himself known, through Israel, to the world. The people of Israel, that is, Jewry, exists only to proclaim this God who has spoken to it.

This God is above all the One God. "Hear (*shema*), O Israel, the Lord our God, the Lord is One"[1] (Deut. 6. 4): that is Israel's primordial act of faith, its supreme prayer, its chief act of witness. This was the purpose of life for countless generations of faithful Israelites and, at need, the purpose of death too, as it was for that Rabbi Akiba, one of Israel's greatest doctors, who died under torture, a victim of the Roman persecution in the second century after Christ, rejoicing in that profession of faith, that act of fidelity and love,

[1] Or, in the spirit of Jewish tradition: "the Lord our God is a unique Lord".

for tradition says that he prolonged the last syllable of the word *ehad* (one, unique) till his last breath. And, says the Talmud, "a voice from heaven was then heard, saying: Blessed art thou, Rabbi Akiba, for thou hast given up thy soul proclaiming my unity; thou shalt have part in the life of the world to come."

Such was the supreme message of Israel, and such it remains. Ever since the synagogue prayers began, the faithful Jew has recited these sacred words three times a day. They constitute the foundation of his religion. What Christ called "the greatest commandment in the Law" (Matt. 22. 36–8) is found, in those very words, in the Old Testament (Deut. 6. 5–6) and in the *Shema* ("Hear, O Israel") of the Jewish prayer, the sequel and the consequence of that proclamation of the divine unity. "Thou shalt love the Lord thy God with the love of thy whole heart, and thy whole soul, and thy whole strength." And indeed, without the absoluteness of this Unity, there could be no total devotion, no undivided service, no real adoration, no true religion. The fundamental importance, and originally most revolutionary character, of this obvious truth are apt to be obscured for us by more than two thousand years of familiarity and intellectual concepts, but for Israel it is nonetheless *the* great revelation, the centre of all its religious life and the historical justification of its existence. Jewish tradition holds that the whole Law simply develops this one and only revelation and works out in detail the manner of serving this One and Only God.

The unity of God which is the basis of Israel's existence and message is neither an abstract unity, such as is conceived by the reasoning of philosophers, nor a mere negation of plurality, arrived at by denying or reducing a number of gods, a process of which there are many examples in history. It is significant that the one foundation of Israel's tradition is the *Torah* ("instruction") in the narrow sense, that is, the Pentateuch, in spite of the explicit and uncompromising message of the One God found in the prophetical books and the vital part played by the prophets in strengthening the monotheistic faith. What is fundamental, in fact, in Jewish monotheism is not the proclamation of a message but the concrete, historical manifestation of the One God, the concrete, historical relations between the One God and his people. Now it is in the Pentateuch that Israel finds this manifestation.

The specific object of Israel's fundamental act of faith is not, in the abstract, the Unity of God but, in the concrete, the One God. Transcendent and personal (as modern language would put it), he is essentially a Living God who, by his Word, created the heavens and the earth, who spoke to Abraham, revealed himself on Sinai, appeared to Isaias, and so on; who constantly addresses man, whom he has created, and constantly intervenes in the history of his people. Unique and transcendent, he is a jealous God, to whom is due all glory and adoration, who has the right to all obedience, to undivided service. There we have one of the immediately obvious "practical" aspects of Israel's fundamental message. In the Semitic languages, "to know God" means to love him, cleave to him, serve him wholly, "walk in his ways". In the Jewish tradition, that is life, salvation, the fulfilment of man's destiny.

It is in this form, in this spirit, that the biblical revelation has been handed down and expressed throughout all Jewish tradition. The Jewish faith is a matter of evidence, founded on the historical experience of God's people, on its dealings with "the God of the fathers", "the God of Abraham, of Isaac and of Jacob" (Exod. 3. 6). This faith is transmitted by a living tradition within the community of the people of God. By his membership of this people, the individual shares in this historical experience and becomes, in a manner, contemporary with the great events of Israel's history: the Exodus, the theophany on Sinai, the conclusion of the Covenant. This faith is so bound up with the historical existence of the people that it may easily give the impression of "fideism" when one tries to formulate it in more abstract terms. At some periods a certain reaction against this appeared, tending to rationalize this faith. Hence, especially in contact with more abstract forms of thought, there was a certain inclination to a monotheism of doctrine instead of a monotheism of life, dwelling rather on the Unity of God than on faith in the One God.[2] We can see it as early as Hellenistic Judaism, or later, for example, in the Arab-Jewish scholasticism of medieval Spain. The anti-Trinitarian controversy, developing over centuries in the setting of debates between Judaism and Christianity, contributed to a certain hardening in the same direction. Together with the Law, the rigorous affirmation of the Unity of God, in a sense which excludes the Christian ideas of the Incarnation and the Trinity, has in fact constituted the rallying-point which has enabled Judaism to resist Christianity and survive. In our day there has appeared a form of liberalism which tends to rationalize Jewish monotheism in a very different sense, going so far as to reduce Judaism to a sort of natural religion, a kind of abstract philosophical deism. Clearly nothing could be more opposed to the true nature and historical reality of Judaism.

To obtain a truer view of the traditional Jewish concept of the One God, we must naturally refer first to the biblical sources, on which the tradition is founded. Here we need only recall some essential features. In Scripture the God of Israel is above all the Most High, the Mighty, awe-inspiring in majesty. He is—and this is one of the names by which rabbinical tradition preferred to address God—"the Holy", "the Holy One of Israel". Abraham, Moses, Isaias, Job, were all overcome with a holy fear in his presence. He dwells in inaccessible light and the manifestation of his glory can destroy the creature. As Creator, he is the absolute Lord of the universe. With a sign, a word, he calls into being the heavens, the earth and the seas. By his sovereign command he gives the waters bounds, which they must not pass. He feeds all living things and if he withholds his breath from

[2] Christian thought encountered the same risk in expressing faith in the Trinity.

them, all fall back into nothingness. There we see some of the major themes of the Prophetical and Sapiential books, and especially of the Psalter, which has always penetrated and nourished Jewish prayer and meditation. We can at once realize an important consequence of this very vivid sense of God the Creator: all that exists is his work, all that exists is therefore fundamentally good, because it comes from him. Judaism has therefore a rooted optimism as to the meaning and values of this world. This is even more valid for man, whom God has created in his likeness in order to place him at the summit of the universe and the hierarchy of beings, and to whom he has given freedom—a moral freedom much emphasized in Jewish thought—so that he may freely serve and praise God. And yet over man, too, God remains absolute Master, the absolute Lord of history as of the universe. He holds in his hands the destinies of his people and of the nations. He bends the hearts of kings to his will. He frees his people from the hands of Pharao when he wills, he drives on the powerful king of Assyria to chastise his people, then, at a stroke, halts him, powerless, before the ramparts of Jerusalem; he summons Cyrus to send back the survivors of his people to Jerusalem. Nothing lies outside his all-powerful operation.

This sense of the divine transcendence grew ever deeper with the development of Israel's religion. Thus it came to eliminate the name of *Yahweh*, the proper, sacred, dread name of the God of Israel, the name revealed to Moses, for according to the Semitic notion the name is part of the mystery of the being who is named. In the third century B.C., *Adonaï* ("our Lord") began to be substituted in public reading for Yahweh: in the Greek version of the Septuagint it was translated by *Kyrios* ("Lord"); in the Aramaic Targums it was often replaced by *Memra* ("Word"), while rabbinical tradition frequently used "the Place", "the Name", "Heaven" (as we find "the kingdom of heaven" for "the kingdom of God" in St Matthew's Gospel), and "the Holy", this last being, as we have seen, the most characteristic. From the Middle Ages, however, Jewish tradition tended to return to the biblical terms, *Elohim* ("God") and *Adonaï* ("our Lord"). In modern Judaism the latter term is often rendered by "the Eternal".

Along with the sense of God's transcendence, the sense of his nearness increased, the feeling of intimacy with him, of a deeply religious familiarity. Many are the psalms which early expressed this element in biblical revelation and impressed it deeply on the Jewish soul. Similarly, in the confidences God entrusted to his spokesmen, to Osee, to Isaias, to Jeremias, we feel an immense tenderness for his children and in particular for his own people. Kindness and mercy appear in many passages of the Bible as the last word of God's manifestation. The primitive terror—which yet did not exclude familiarity, as we see with Abraham, for example—is thus more and more transformed into filial fear. God reveals himself more and more as a Father to his people, but also to each one of his faithful and to all men. It is not only his sacred majesty and his tremendous power which are praised but equally, and even more, the God who is "the merciful, the gracious, slow to take vengeance, rich in kindness, faithful to his promises" (Exod. 34. 6).

The synthesis of the two elements was finally achieved in later Judaism. In prayer, which best expresses the tonality of the relations between man and God, the terms mentioned above give way more and more to the words "our Father" and "our King". And although in certain periods, especially the first Christian centuries, there was still some reaction against anthropomorphic terms which might have tarnished the sentiment of God's transcendence, we see that at other times, both in talmudic tradition and in later trends, the doctors and spiritual guides of Israel can still use these terms without scruple, to speak of the living God and to speak to him. Among the later trends,[3] each of which reveals an element in the Jewish soul and enriches Jewish tradition by its contribution, speculations of the Cabbalistic type placed the accent rather on the divine transcendence, while the piety

[3] Cf. Chapter VI.

nourished on the Psalter and Haggadic tradition, like that of the *Chasidim*, emphasized above all the intimacy, the familiar converse with the Eternal.

The attitude of the faithful Israelite to his God, in all its varying aspects, reflects the image of God as it is presented in the whole of revelation and the tradition of Israel. To the justice of God, which is demanded by his holiness, corresponds fear, a fear fundamentally religious. To his mercy, to his unwearying and paternal kindness, corresponds love. The talmudic tradition, faithful in this to the biblical tradition, while always insisting on the wholesome value of the fear of God, not a primitive terror, but an awareness of the gulf separating sinful man from the holiness demanded and called for by the Holiness of God, sets love above fear, or rather, sees the fear of God as a fear inspired by love. It is entirely in this sense that in the Bible the fear of God—for example, the fear which inspired Abraham not to refuse his only son to the Lord—is represented as a summary of all the commandments and the beginning of wisdom. It leads one to "walk in the ways of the Lord"; it is an entire submission to his will. It corresponds roughly to what Catholic theology calls the virtue of religion. It is the fundamental attitude of the creature to his Creator, compounded of adoration, submission and devotedness, in a person-to-person relationship in which God and his creature are both infinitely distant and infinitely near. Fear of this sort means, in the last resort, "to love God with the love of the whole heart, the whole mind and the whole strength". Nothing could be more inaccurate or unjust than to contrast—whether out of controversial distortion, unconscious Gnosticism, anti-Jewish prejudice or simple ignorance —the God of the New Testament with the God of the Old, as a God of Love with a God of Fear (or Anger, or even Revenge), or to contrast Christianity with Judaism as a religion of love with a religion of justice or fear. It would be completely to misunderstand what is really new in the teaching, the person and the work of Christ, and how he came "not to destroy but to fulfil" (Matt. 5. 17).

The filial fear of God which marks the spirit of Judaism flowers quite naturally into joy, a joy which often irradiates the souls of the devout in Israel and constantly shines out in the synagogue prayers. It transfigures the most meticulous observances of the Law, through the certitude that thereby God is being served as he wishes to be served. Disinterested love, and the joy which flows from it, seek to blaze a freer trail, beyond the rigours of all kinds of legalism, in the mystical trends which we describe in our sixth chapter.

It is in prayer, in the words of the synagogue liturgy, that we find the Jewish concept of the relations between God and man most faithfully expressed. The sense of sin and the longing for pardon, with the plaintive notes of supplication, expectation and appeal for help, are frequently expressed, but the dominant note is always that of filial trust, overflowing in joy and of gratitude which never wearies of telling the benefits and the promises of the Lord to his people. The historical dimensions of the Jewish faith are always present in prayer, which yet aspires to the heights of a prayer which is above all that is contingent and particular. These two sentiments, trust and gratitude, are expressed above all in a prayer of praise and blessing ("blessing" in the sense it has in Judaism, a prayer of praise and thanksgiving).

We can best illustrate the true Jewish doctrine of the living God, not by the standards of an elaborated Jewish theology (which would not differ greatly from the treatise *De Deo Uno* in scholastic theology), nor by the standards of rabbinical theology (which generally only underline at one time some aspect or other of the faith of Judaism), but by some passages from the synagogue prayers. Take, for example, the beginning of the Prayer (*Tephillah*) *par excellence,* the "Prayer of the Eighteen Blessings" (*Shemoneh-Esreh*), one of the oldest and fullest prayers of this liturgy, which the faithful Jew recites every day, in public and in private:

> Blessed art thou, O Lord our God and God of our fathers, God of Abraham, God of Isaac and God of Jacob, the great, mighty and revered God, the most high God, who bestowest

lovingkindnesses, and possessest all things; who rememberest the pious deeds of the patriarchs, and in love wilt bring a redeemer to their children's children for thy name's sake. O King, Helper, Saviour and Shield. Blessed art thou, O Lord, the Shield of Abraham.

Thou, O Lord, art mighty for ever, thou quickenest the dead, thou art mighty to save. Thou sustainest the living with lovingkindness, quickenest the dead with great mercy, supportest the failing, healest the sick, loosest the bound, and keepest thy faith to them that sleep in the dust. Who is like unto thee, Lord of mighty acts, and who resembleth thee? . . . Blessed art thou, O Lord, who quickenest the dead.

Thou art holy, and thy name is holy, and holy beings praise thee daily. Blessed art thou, O Lord, the holy God. . . .

Cause us to return, O our Father, unto thy Law . . . bring us back in perfect repentance unto thy presence. Blessed art thou, O Lord, who delightest in repentance.

Forgive us, O our Father, for we have sinned; pardon us, O our King, for we have transgressed; for thou dost pardon and forgive. Blessed art thou, O Lord, who art gracious, and dost abundantly forgive.

This other example is taken from the *Kedushah*, inserted every day in the "Eighteen Blessings":

Unto all generations we will declare thy greatness, and to all eternity we will proclaim thy holiness, and thy praise, O our God, shall not depart from our mouth for ever, for thou art a great and holy God and King. Blessed art thou, O Lord, the holy God.

THE PEOPLE OF GOD

In the introduction to the Jewish doctrine of God, emphasis was laid on the essential relation between God and the people which he raised up, chose and educated to be his spokesman and witness among mankind. This means that in its own eyes —and also in the Christian's, though from a new angle—Israel has a primordial religious significance, inherent in its existence. Israel believes itself to be a fact of theology as much as of history, since its history is itself "theophorous", bearing

God within it. Accordingly, having outlined Israel's faith in the One God, we must at once turn to the people itself, which has received the revelation of this One God, guards it and testifies to it.

This unique rôle of Israel's arises from a divine choice, a choice which makes Israel God's people: "I will be your God, and you shall be my people." The choice is what establishes the people of God. It is the primary fact, the first intervention on God's part, the creative act which raises up the people through whom God will unfold his saving design in history. In the biblical tradition, God's "election" of Israel appears as an action free and undeserved, an act of "prevenient love", for which continual thanksgiving is due. Even if there is often mention of the promises made to the patriarchs, and the faithfulness of these fathers of the chosen people, these "claims" are connected with God's later gifts, the deliverance from Egypt, the Covenant, etc., but never with the first choice, which is earlier than them. In rabbinical tradition, indeed, we find speculations about some sort of reciprocity between God's choice and that of the patriarchs, or about the choice being first offered to other peoples and refused by them before being offered to Israel and accepted by it. These speculations testify to the existence in Jewish tradition of a current which rather tends to obscure the absolute freedom of the divine choice, but other texts, and especially the words of the prayers, show that these speculations have not seriously affected belief in this free choice.

As man has been placed by the Creator at the summit of the hierarchy of beings, to acknowledge, praise and serve God in the name of all creation, so the chosen people is placed at the summit or centre of mankind, there to be God's witness and servant, a holy people and a nation of priests, charged with praising God in the name of all mankind, of the whole world.

The choice is revealed first by a call and a promise, addressed to the future people of God in the person of its first father, Abraham. It was carried out in the destiny of

Abraham's posterity and in the historical formation of the people of Israel. It was eventually defined in a precise and (for Israel) final way, in the Covenant, first in the Covenant made by God with Abraham, but above all in the Covenant made on Sinai through the mediation of Moses.

The Covenant is inseparable from the revelation of the One God and from the promulgation of the Law, which was to be the charter of the Covenant. From another angle, it is inseparable from the Exodus and the deliverance from Egypt. For all Jewish tradition, this deliverance is the central event of Israel's history. It constitutes the first fulfilment of the promise to Abraham, the pledge, for the future, of the unshakable fidelity of God the Saviour towards his people, the immediate preparation for the inauguration of the Covenant, and finally the prefiguring of the consummation, the ultimate Messianic deliverance. Out of Egypt God leads his liberated people into the desert in order, as it were, to educate them, and to inaugurate at Sinai the Covenant which will decisively make, out of a still formless mass of tribes, a real people, a real people of God. These events, the deliverance, the Exodus, the inauguration of the Covenant and the giving of the Law, are all one thing in Jewish tradition, together constituting the starting-point, the centre, the summit, the source whence flows the whole existence of the people of God.

To this event the prayer and meditation of Israel constantly return, here to find their spiritual food; here the research and speculation of the rabbis turn, to find their foundations. A stage was reached—as has been already noted—when all revelation and all authentic tradition, written or oral, was ascribed to Sinai, rejecting the idea of any later addition, any progressive revelation, and at the same time (though this was certainly late, and partly in reaction against Christian arguments) the strictly Mosaic origin of the Pentateuch was made a sort of fundamental dogma, leaving to the prophets and the other inspired Scriptures only the rôle of recalling, applying and interpreting the revelation of the laws contained in the Torah.

In Jewish tradition the Covenant of Sinai is thought of both as a free gift and as a bilateral engagement. The free gift derives from the choice, the promise, the faithfulness of God. This was the aspect emphasized by Hellenistic Jewish thought, which in the Septuagint renders the Hebrew *berit* by the Greek *diatheke* (a unilateral disposition, a will), whereas St Paul emphasizes the bilateral aspect of the Covenant, the better to contrast it with the free Promise made to Abraham and fulfilled in Christ. In the tradition of rabbinical Judaism, the aspect of the free gift is applied above all to the Law, while the Covenant is generally viewed under its bilateral aspect.

But to Jewish tradition, as to Deuteronomy, the Covenant is not only bilateral; it is also, in principal, conditional. Israel is pledged to remain faithful to the Lord and to observe his commandments, while the Lord engages to protect, guide and reward his people, *if it is faithful*. In this way the permanence of the Covenant testified, in the eyes of the rabbis, both to the unshakable and merciful faithfulness of the God of Sinai, and to the essential faithfulness of the people—which does not exclude countless temporary infidelities on its part.

The Law defines the Covenant's demands, and is thus the test of Israel's faithfulness to the Covenant. According to an ancient *midrash*, the Israelite who breaks the Law violates the Covenant. We must remember in this connection that the fundamentally corporate nature of Jewish religious life derives from the fact that the object of the choice and the Covenant is the people as such, and the individual shares in them only as a member of the people, the *kahal* (assembly, convocation) of Israel. Circumcision and the Sabbath, among other things, are the signs of the Covenant, of membership of the Covenant. The Law, with its countless commandments, is the proof that from the Covenant there flow down from God to Israel not only a unique tenderness and solicitude, but also a unique call to faithfulness and holiness: God is always ready to load his people with favours and to pardon it whenever it returns to him, but also to prove and chastise it whenever it shows itself unfaithful to the Law and the Covenant.

Finally, in its fundamental union with the People and the Law, the Covenant comprises a third element, which in a way is a constituent of it: the promised Land, the Land of Israel. This Land is the tangible and primary object of God's promise, both in Abraham's day and at the time of Sinai. It is an intrinsic part of the life of the nation of Israel, and the Law, which is to govern the life of God's people, is connected in many ways with life in the promised Land. In rabbinical doctrine, moreover, the observance of the Law in the Land has a special significance and value, and it can never be perfect in a foreign land. With Israel in exile, the *shechinah* itself—the presence of God's glory—is in exile. This part played by the Land in God's designs enters equally into Judaism's Messianic and eschatological hopes, in which the return to the promised Land and the complete restoration of the people of God in its own land hold an important place. For this reason, throughout all the long ages of dispersion, Judaism has always been spiritually turned towards Jerusalem and the promised Land. The place of the Land in Judaism's horizons, far from being a purely national factor, has a religious bearing, closely bound up with the Covenant, and so with the very nature of the people of Israel.[4]

Such, then, in Jewish tradition, are the main aspects of the very special and close bond established between God and Israel by the Covenant. The consciousness of this bond is deeply rooted in the Jewish soul, and there is no manifestation of Jewish life in which it is not to some degree present. It is present in the sentiment of the grandeur, the nobility of Israel's rôle and equally in that of the burden of the divine demands, the arduous condition which that rôle involves.

[4] It is therefore understandable that the Zionist achievement, the creation of the State of Israel, evokes a profound response and mobilizes forces which are vital in the heart of Judaism, but it can have only a distant, if not deceptive, proportion and connection with its essential hopes.

The whole Jewish view of the history and destiny of the people is founded on the Covenant, its demands and its promises. It is in the light of this central event that Jewish tradition sees the meaning of the captivities and deliverances, the exiles and returns, the dispersions and the reunions, the infidelities and the repentances, the graces and the trials of the past, the present and the future of God's people, down to the final deliverance and reunion foretold by the prophets. In medieval Jewish thought, the original Exile—the *galut*—was given the meaning of a purifying trial, expiating and redeeming, and the Dispersion, of course, had long been recognized as a providential condition for the diffusion of the knowledge of the One God among the nations.

The mission of God's people is in fact twofold. In the Bible and early Judaism this mission is above all to be a witness to the living God, a witness to his word and his favours, as much by its historical existence as by its fidelity to his Law. Then, reflecting on the revelation given to it and on its own history, Jewish tradition brought to light another aspect of this mission: Israel is the servant of God: the "Servant poems" in the second part of the book of Isaias are often interpreted in this sense in Jewish tradition. Its task is to work for the establishment of the Kingdom, to hasten the coming of the Messiah and the final consummation: to be a servant, not only by the witness of its faith and fidelity, but also by its prayer and the redemptive value of its fidelities, and above all of its sufferings, notably those of its exile. The trials of the Middle Ages, indirect Christian influences, the cessation of the active testimony of proselytism, and finally the speculations of the Cabbalah, no doubt all contributed to emphasize the second of these two complementary aspects of Israel's mission.

But under these two aspects, it is fidelity to the Law, and thereby to the Covenant, that is the condition of the fulfilment of the mission of God's people. According to a *midrash* on Exodus, "When the Israelites do the will of *the Place* (i.e. of God), his Name is exalted in the world . . . but when they do not his will, his Name is profaned in the world." The fidelity or infidelity of every Israelite reacts on the community, retains or repels the *shechinah* and contributes to hastening or delaying the coming of the Messiah.

This mission, like the election and the Covenant, belongs to Israel alone. While the knowledge of God and the moral law are for all the nations, for all men—and Israel's mission is precisely to make them known to all—the obligation of the whole Torah, "the yoke of the Kingdom", remains the onerous but glorious privilege of the chosen people, whose mission requires a special "holiness" and a separation from the other nations.

In the centuries before and after the birth of Christianity, in the Jewish world proselytism was generally considered to form part of the mission of testimony entrusted to Israel. But after the slackening and almost complete cessation of proselytism, it came to be regarded in the Middle Ages as not forming part of that mission, and quite often was even viewed with a certain mistrust. This attitude is now beginning to be questioned in some Jewish circles, notably in those of Liberal tendencies, and especially in countries, like the United States, where conversions to Judaism are comparatively frequent.

The expansion of Christianity and Islam naturally had much to do with the cessation of Jewish proselytism and the development of Jewish ideas about the duty of it. The great Jewish thinkers of the Middle Ages came to think that the Church and Islam had adapted and handed on to the nations the essence of the biblical message and its moral law (formulated in the Decalogue), and were therefore playing a providential rôle, in this capacity, in the preparation for the Kingdom of God, so carrying on the rôle of Israel. This of course did not prevent Judaism from firmly maintaining its position as the one people of God, sole depositary of the authentic and complete revelation, nor from rejecting everything in Christian or Moslem doctrine which appeared incompatible with its own teaching, ascribing it to corruptions of pagan origin. Some isolated thinkers and writers of the Liberal movement would nowadays tend to go further and allow Christianity to have a genuine mission of salvation—and Jesus to have a sort of authentic Messianic mission—for the benefit of the pagan nations, parallel with Israel's mission. But such ideas can really only aggravate the difficulty which Jewish thought is already experiencing to its cost, that of reconciling the universalist and particularist aspects of its tradition.

This sketch of Judaism's concept of itself and its mission shows clearly enough that all Jewish tradition, biblical and post-biblical, involves a certain duality, a certain tension between the factors of universalism and those of particularism. The former are more fundamental and constantly appear in rabbinical literature, especially its moral teaching, but the latter are often more in evidence and seem to be inherent in all that is exclusive in the election, the Covenant, the Law and the special mission of Israel, so that they can never be transcended within the setting of Judaism. Even in the realm of Messianic expectations, the possibility of considering not only the Jews but all mankind in a fully universal vision has always been something uncertain and debatable in Judaism. That, as we know, was one of the roots of the schism between the community of Israel and the infant Church.

If many Jews and many trends in Jewish thought and tradition have yielded to the narrower view, to the temptation to be complacent about their election, their privileges and the greatness of their rôle, we should be the last to be shocked or surprised at it, since in spite of the total and explicit universalism of the Church and the Christian message, we know that in Christianity itself there has often been little resistance to this very human temptation. And the Christian, of all people, ought to understand that the particularism contained in Judaism, and that by the will of God himself, could not be transcended and fully integrated into the fundamental universalism of God's design, except in Christ.[5]

THE RELIGION OF THE TORAH

In the preceding pages there has already been frequent mention of the Torah, of the meaning and content of the term, of the place of the Torah in revelation, of its connection with the Covenant, of its transmission and interpretation, etc. Nevertheless, if we are to understand the soul, the nature and the structure of Judaism, we must again return to the Torah and try to throw more light on its place in Jewish life.

This place is so central that all the various trends, forms of thought or spirituality, and all the schisms in Judaism, are distinguished with reference to the Torah, just as Judaism is distinguished by the Torah from all other religions, and especially from Christianity. As was shown in Chapter II, all Jewish tradition, all rabbinical tradition, has been formed around the Torah and is grafted on it in its entirety. In the here and now of everyday life it is the Torah which objectifies all God's favours to his people: the gift of the Torah is thus seen as God's gift *par excellence*. Constantly, in its prayer, Israel proclaims its gratitude for this gift, as in this blessing pronounced in the synagogue before the reading of the Torah: "Blessed art thou, O Lord our God, King of the universe, who hast chosen us from all nations and given us thy Law, Blessed art thou, O Lord, who givest the Law."

As early as the last centuries of the biblical era, the unrivalled esteem in which the Torah was held had given rise to a veneration, a regular devotion to it. The typical expression

[5] That is what St Paul so well expresses when, fully in the line of Jewish tradition, he recounts all the privileges which set Israel apart among the nations, but adds precisely the supreme Gift given to Israel: Christ, in whom Israel's destiny opens on prospects now entirely universalist: "They are Israelites, adopted as God's sons; the visible presence, and the covenant, and the giving of the law, and the Temple worship, and the promises, are their inheritance; the patriarchs belong to them, and theirs is the human stock from which Christ came; Christ, who rules as God over all things, blessed for ever, Amen" (Rom. 9. 4–5).

of this is found in Psalm 118 (119), but also in the Wisdom books and extra-biblical literature, such as the older parts of the Mishnah. This devotion tends to personify the Torah, to identify it with Wisdom, to ascribe to it pre-existence in the presence of God and to make it one of the foundations of creation. The speculations of the Cabbalists gave these ideas some subtle and often strange developments. The place held in the synagogue by the solemn reading of the Torah and the actual scrolls of the Torah, and by the liturgical honours accorded to them, are eloquent testimony to this veneration, and so is the devout and minutely regulated care given to the making of the scrolls.

According to a pronouncement going back to the *tannaim* of the second century, when God said to Israel in Exod. 19. 5, "You shall be my own", this meant: "You shall be turned towards me and busy with the words of the Torah, not taken up with any other affairs." The whole life of Judaism has in fact always revolved about the Torah, its study and its observance.

The value attached in traditional Judaism to the study of the Torah, which is a *duty* for every Israelite, is a significant proof of its central place in Jewish life. If this zeal for the study of the Law has also given rise to some exaggerations—which is only human—that does not alter the importance of the fact. In no other people, no other religion can we find anything comparable to this immense labour of study, pursued through the ages by so great a number of the faithful throughout their lives and finally, in these latter ages, by practically the entire male population of vast communities of traditional Ashkenazim, often at the cost of great sacrifice. Despite the dangers of narrowness and formalism, which beset every scholastic tradition and all excessive specialization, this vast enterprise of study has been able, on the whole, to keep the spirit of the religion of the Torah and has not lost sight of its aim: not a mere theoretical knowledge of the Torah, but a more exact, faithful and perfect performance of its precepts, which are "a way which leads to life", to justice, to holiness. Even in the most subtle or abstract discussion the aim is always action, the practice, application and observance of the Law of God. In a characteristic passage of the Talmud we read of a discussion at Lydda, on the question: which is the more important, study or practice? "Rabbi Tarphon replied: It is practice. But Rabbi Akiba answered: It is study. Finally all agreed that study was the greater, for study leads to action." The same priority of aims is found in this prayer in the Jewish Ritual: "Our Father, who art a Father full of mercy, have pity on us and make our hearts apt to understand, to know and to listen, to learn and to teach, to observe and lovingly practise all the words of the Torah."

The tradition of teaching centred on the Torah is thus fundamentally practical, directed towards action. Neither speculative mystics nor genuine contemplatives have been lacking in the history of Judaism, but neither the one nor the other have modified this practical attitude, looking to action, to life. Faith, to a Jew, is primarily a submission to the God who commands and a trust in the God who promises, rather than a source of contemplation or a seed of the vision of God. The idea of mystery and the corresponding idea of dogma are foreign to Judaism, and its theological research is directed to the systematization, application and explanation of a law of life, rather than to the intellectual exploration of a revealed deposit. The problem of the relation between "faith" and "works" does not arise in Judaism. From the very nature of the Torah, which is its centre, Jewish faith can only fully exist when it is embodied in the "works" of the Law.

The "observances" of the Law, these *mitzvot*,[6] which are the subject of the next section, are therefore not something external to the Jewish religion; they are of the very essence of that religion of the Torah, which cannot exist except as embodied in the daily life of a people, a people which is what it is, only by the continual observance of the Law.

[6] Plural of *mitzvah*, a word meaning both "commandment" and "fulfilment of a commandment", or a "work" in the theological sense, or even a "good work".

To understand the religious values of the Jewish "observances" we must never forget that these observances largely relate to prayer, to the "blessings" by which the pious Jew must hallow all the actions of his life, and to the "service" *par excellence*, the praise of God, the synagogue services. It is only for the sake of clarity that we treat of the synagogue liturgy separately from the other observances of the Law.

The vital rôle of the observances in Judaism has often caused it to be accused of legalism and formalism. The biblical prophets had to stand out against this danger and the doctors of Israel have never ceased to echo their protests. This danger is inherent in the very nature of every institutional religion which has a legal and ritual framework. It would be absurd to claim that Judaism has always escaped this danger, as it would be unjust to assert that it has yielded to it generally or decisively. What is decisive in this connection is not the greater or smaller part which rites and observances play in a religion, but the living faith, the real fervour which animates their performance and gives them their religious meaning and value. If we are to gain a true comprehension, from this point of view, of the manifestations of Jewish life, we must obviously have a sufficient understanding of the true nature of Judaism as a "religion of the Torah".[7]

THE OBSERVANCES OF THE LAW

The nature of these "observances", their meaning and place in Jewish life, have been indicated in the preceding sections. The tendency to develop and multiply them flows precisely from that place and that meaning. It is by faithfully observing

[7] In our day especially, we must beware of judging Judaism by the impression which may be given, not by live and fervent communities, but by Jewish individuals or groups in which the living soul of Judaism is extinct or almost so, but where, by force of habit, the "practices" still survive, at least in part, deprived of their spirit. That would be just as mistaken and unjust as it would be to judge the Church by the behaviour of Catholic communities who, out of habit and inertia, still keep up a certain routine "practice" which (at least in appearance) is not animated by any living faith.

the precepts of the Law that the Israelite renews the Covenant and accomplishes Israel's mission. Now the rôle of the Covenant and the Torah is not confined to certain moments of life; it covers its whole extent. Nothing, then, can be more logical, from this point of view, than to multiply the prescriptions so as to enclose the whole life of the individual, the family, the community, the whole people, in a network of observances, in order to make every movement, every action, a fulfilment of the Law, a *mitzvah*, and thus to consecrate, as it should be, the whole life of Israel and the Israelite, from birth till death. The consequent proliferation and minuteness would seem fatally strange if we did not view them in their context and with their religious content.

But whence have these prescriptions been drawn, so numerous that they can frame, regulate and sanctify every moment of life? They are drawn, naturally, from the Torah, not only from the written Torah, but also—as was noted in Chapter II—from the oral Torah, that is, from the living and authentic tradition of God's people. From the *halachic* tradition, too, which finds in the Torah and the other sources of tradition practical interpretations and obligatory rules of conduct, believed to go back to Moses, to Sinai, and to derive thence their authority and binding force. The agelong activity of the doctors, the academies, the schools, the rabbinical tribunals, the authors or compilers of the great collections and codifications, has no other aim than to transmit the whole Torah and its precepts, to define and ensure their observance as perfectly as possible. To this end, they strove to determine how the different commandments of the Torah should be applied in different circumstances, to surround them with a protecting hedge, formed of supplementary precepts designed to eliminate all danger of transgression, and finally to avoid the multiplication of sins, by so interpreting the commandments as to lighten the burden which might have become too heavy for the people. As in all fields of law and jurisprudence, this legal activity could easily go astray, whether towards a certain legalist rigour or towards a casuistry of the opposite tendency. In the rabbinical literature itself, both these deviations are severely criticized.

The multiplicity of precepts, however, was not without its drawbacks: it was apt to bewilder and dissipate the efforts of the faithful. And so, as early as Hillel, who had summed up the whole Law in the love of one's neighbour, many attempts were made to introduce some general principles and a hierarchy of values in the laws, so as to give them a certain unity. It was this same need for order and clarity which called forth the later codifications. But in the beginnings of rabbinical tradition a count had been made of the precepts contained in the Law and a list was established, which was to become classic, comprising 613 precepts, 248 of which were positive and 365 negative. As regards their subject-matter, these precepts are obviously of unequal importance, and the rabbis themselves often classified them according to an order of gravity. But in so far as they are *mitzvot*, fulfilments of the Law, they have all the same religious value and are all mutually dependent, since the common aim of them all is the accomplishment of the whole Torah.

Yet the religious value of the *mitzvot* does not depend on the mere outward performance of the precepts of the Law. The need to ward off the danger of formalism has led Jewish tradition to discern and clearly formulate what it is that constitutes the profound unity and religious value of these numerous observances: it is the intention, the *kavannah* or religious intention, with the motives which inspire it.

The doctrine of the *kavannah* plays an important part in all Jewish spirituality, and tradition has always set before the Israelite the highest and most disinterested motives for his actions and observances: to fulfil the Law in some way for its own sake, because it is God's will, in God's sight, and to be faithful to the engagement accepted by Israel at the inauguration of the Covenant. Still more fundamentally, the precepts of the Law must be carried out in order to attain the purpose of Israel's election, which is to hallow the Name, to glorify God and bear witness to him before the world, to hasten the coming of the Kingdom of God, in which the Lord's Name will be fully glorified. Many are the passages in rabbinical literature which insist on lofty motives and disinterestedness in the observance of the commandments, or recall striking examples of really disinterested love in the fulfilment of the Law. In Chasidism, this theme is extraordinarily prominent. It is this disinterestedness of the genuine *kavannah* which, to the fervent Israelite, transforms into joy what to others might seem a yoke and a burden.

Besides this quest of a pure and disinterested fidelity, rabbinical tradition, like Catholic theology, is also familiar with the notion of merit (*zechut*). This is, in fact, simply the accomplished *mitzvah* which endures and, while it hastens the coming of the Kingdom, also purifies and sanctifies the one who has performed it, and constitutes a ground of reward in him. But the more precise formulation of a doctrine of merit and reward has come up against difficulties in Judaism, analogous to those experienced in this domain by Christian thought.

After these general remarks on observances in Judaism, one may ask to what subjects these numerous observances, commandments and precepts of the Torah apply. We may distinguish two main categories: the sphere of worship and that of morality. The former includes not only prayer and the liturgy but also all those *mitzvot* which concern worship, everything connected with the sanctification of persons, occasions of life, activities or objects. The latter concerns the behaviour of man towards his fellows, towards himself and the things of this world. But between these two spheres there is no separation, no clearly drawn frontier. In each, it is a matter of carrying out the Torah, doing the will of God. In Israel, a people dedicated to the service of God, every act of worship also concerns morals, and every act of a moral nature is related to worship. While we study separately some characteristic traits of Jewish ethics (in the next section) and the principal forms of worship (in Chapter V), it will be well to bear this unity in mind.

JEWISH MORAL TEACHING

The considerations here set forth will have helped us to understand the organic function of the moral teaching of Judaism in Jewish life as a whole, notably in relation to the Torah. The chief aim of the remarks which now follow is to throw light on the foundations of Jewish moral teaching, not from the point of view of the Law of God, but from that of the nature and will of man, and to point out some characteristic features of that teaching.

Any concept of moral values is based on a concept of man. That of Judaism is directly derived from the biblical doctrine of creation. Creation, being the work of God, is fundamentally good and is an organic unity. In Judaism, neither the experience of human divisions and frailties, nor the seductions of Manichean ideas and dualist philosophies have ever been able seriously to impair a concept of man which is fundamentally optimistic and fundamentally unitary. This concept is both cosmic and moral: it is aware of both the greatness and the misery of man's condition, which is so exactly reflected, in its most acute form, in the condition of the Jew, squarely faced with the clearest and most exacting expression of God's will, the Torah, and thereby charged with a very special responsibility.

The idea of responsibility and freedom is at the heart of the Jewish concept of man and morality. Judaism knows that man is feeble, that he is but "flesh", a creature, fragile, limited, divided. Rabbinical tradition hesitated for a time between several ideas of man's condition, some of which were not far from the doctrine of original sin. But partly, no doubt, in reaction against that Christian doctrine, so bound up with the doctrine of Christ the Redeemer, it finally inclined to a more radically optimistic concept of man's nature and liberty. Yet Judaism preserved from its biblical heritage a doctrine of grace—*chesed*—(without trying to formulate a theology of grace) and a lively sentiment of the penetrating action of an all-powerful Providence. But in their care for a rigorous education of the moral sense, and in reaction against the Christian concept of grace and against Moslem fatalism, Jewish thinkers and doctors were led to insist strongly, sometimes exclusively, on man's entire liberty of choice, "placed in presence of life and death", of good and evil. They acknowledge, indeed, a "bad tendency" in man, as well as a "good tendency", but firmly maintain that man, in spite of all the limitations he is helpless to remove, can always choose the good, with the lights of the Law and his conscience, and with help from on high which leaves his freedom intact. According to a talmudic saying, "At a man's birth, God decides if he will be weak or strong, wise or foolish, rich or poor, but not if he will be good or bad." As the whole of Jewish life has assumed the form of a saving observance, outside of which is nothing but culpable transgression, this insistence on man's freedom and responsibility is only natural.

The Jewish idea of creation likewise results in a historical and cosmic optimism, a profound appreciation of created values and an instinctive trust in the destinies of man and the world. Although the vicissitudes of history have not usually been favourable to these tendencies, it is a fact that Jewish tradition contains the roots of a humanism and a dynamism of progress which have found their expression, paradoxically, at the present day, just where the tradition which transmitted them was beginning to decline.

The same concept of human nature explains the theoretically somewhat inferior place held by asceticism in Jewish spirituality. But from this point of view the contrast with Christianity is perhaps more apparent than real. The Law itself, with its observances—which in many ways makes the life of the pious Jew not unlike that of the Christian monk or nun—imposes on the faithful a very real asceticism, of which other manifestations are found in various trends of Jewish spirituality. But we should obviously not expect to find in Judaism the ascetical *ideas* which are founded on specifically Christian considerations, such as the cross of Christ.

The moral teaching of Judaism comprises a precise conception of sin, which necessarily holds an important place in it. The will of God for Israel and mankind being embodied in the Law, it is by the Law that sin is essentially defined. It is conceived above all as a transgression, a disobedience, a revolt against God, "King of the world", as the Jewish liturgy often calls him. For Israel itself, however, sin finds its full significance only in the historical context of salvation. The consequences of sin are diametrically opposite to those of the *mitzvah*. It violates the Covenant, banishes the *shechinah*, the divine presence, profanes the Name of God before the nations and delays the coming of the Kingdom. Moreover, until it is effaced, it remains, as an accomplished act, in the one who has committed it, as a ground of punishment—just as the *mitzvah* is a ground of reward. The sense of sin, the desire to be freed from it, and prayer for pardon hold an important place in Jewish spirituality and liturgical prayer. They are specially prominent in the offices of the Day of Atonement, which are very elaborate. The sacrifices for sin, having come to an end, have been replaced by prayer and other works of penitence and expiation, such as fasting, alms-giving and the acceptance of trials. But the essential condition of pardon is always *teshuvah*, the conversion of the heart, by which the sinner, who of his own free will has turned away from God, turns back to him with sincere repentance. The Jew who has been brought up on the Scriptures is not likely to forget that this repentance, this turning back, is a grace: in his prayer he never ceases to beseech God to give him a contrite heart and draw him back to him.

Further disquisition on the rules of Jewish morality would not be very interesting, for being founded on the Decalogue they have that common ground with Christian morality, and indeed are practically identical with "natural" morality. According to the explicit teaching of the masters of Israel, this fundamental part of morality and the Law has of its nature a universal bearing, binding on the nations as well as on Israel. Some talmudic sayings, and also modern Jewish thought, tend to attach these moral precepts to the Covenant granted by God to Noah after the flood for all post-diluvian mankind.

Among the principles of Jewish morality which are both natural and positive, there are some domains which certainly deserve special attention, because of their importance and significant features. One is the family, and we know that from biblical times to our own day, family life in the Jewish world has preserved its characteristic importance and intensity. Another is marriage, for though Judaism admits divorce it is, in principle, only unwillingly, and with meticulous legislation to restrict it to grave cases. There is respect for woman and her rôle in society, for while the study of the Law and active participation in public worship are reserved to men, woman occupies a prominent place in domestic worship and the whole of family life. The moral concepts of Judaism have been strongly marked by other aspects of biblical tradition, such as a very great respect for human life. A passionate vindication of justice—a justice essentially religious, but at the same time profoundly human and social—was, of course, one of the most constant and revolutionary themes of the message of the prophets of Israel. This "hunger and thirst after justice" has always been a very living thing in Judaism. It is expressed in countless passages of legislation and rabbinical teaching and has so impregnated Jewish sentiment that even after the decline of the traditional influences in emancipated Judaism it has remained one of the most characteristic features to receive the support of Jewry in the modern world. And this support is the more important in that the Jewish concept of justice, as of all morality, is still fundamentally corporate, and thus provides a useful counterbalance to the sometimes too purely individualist tendencies which have prevailed in Christian countries of our time.

But we must not reduce the moral and social meaning of Jewish justice—*tzedakah*—to the much more limited sense covered by the word in modern languages. *Tzedakah* is a much wider and deeper idea and more directly religious, for in the last resort it is always connected with God and makes one "just" in God's sight. In all tradition it is closely connected with the idea of *mitzvah*: it is a carrying out of the Law, that is, of the will of God. The meaning of *tzaddik*, the just, in Judaism is very like that of "saint" in Christian usage. At the same time, *tzedakah* always relates to man, to the "neighbour": it means kindness, love, charity (sometimes, as in English, with the restricted sense of almsgiving). It is characteristic of Judaism never to separate justice and love, whether towards God or towards man. The two, which are therefore only one, are moreover conceived, practised and (in Jewish communities) organized in a way which is both personal and corporate. Jewish tradition often insists on the respect due to the "neighbour" and especially to the "poor", and on the altruism necessary in the exercise of charity, which is at the same time a duty of justice to God. If the accent is sometimes different from that which has prevailed in Christian tradition, in the light of the teaching and example of Christ, it must never be forgotten that the "second commandment", which is "like the first" (Matt. 22. 39), the command to love one's neighbour, is already found in the Old Testament (Levit. 19. 18), the common patrimony of Israel and the Church. Jewish teaching has never lost sight of the capital importance and universal application of this great commandment. In its theological outlook it may have had difficulty in expressing the universal bearing of its mission, but in the field of morals, and notably as regards the love of one's neighbour, even though some rabbinical texts suggest a more particularist view, Jewish tradition has in the main been able to preserve its universalist inspiration.

ISRAEL'S HOPE

In the foregoing sketch of Israel's vision of its own destinies and those of the world, the question of its hopes has barely been touched upon. But the picture of the main lines of Jewish doctrine would be gravely incomplete if, to conclude this chapter, the vital part these hopes play in the life and teaching of Judaism were not dealt with at greater length.

They form, in fact, a central theme, continually recurring in Israel's prayer; it holds an important place in the discussions of the rabbis; it dominates the Jewish view of history; above all, it marks the whole of Jewish tradition with the note of an expectation, an aspiration, an ardent hope, which has been and still remains one of the deepest sources of its vitality and spirituality. There is scarcely any formulated synthesis of it, no elaborated theology. It is in the depths of Jewish tradition and the daily expression of its life, and especially its prayer, that we can perceive the chief marks of its hope. There is inevitably something arbitrary about distinguishing different elements in the living sheaf of this hope, but the complexity of the subject makes this method necessary. In this hope, then, we shall distinguish three aspects: the more general expectation of the Kingdom of God, the strictly Messianic expectation, and the hope of "the world to come". The first two are contained in the dimension of history, whereas the third looks to the end of time and the things beyond time.

The expectation of the Kingdom

The attitude of expectation is fundamental in Israel's life. It penetrates deep into its history, its tradition, its soul. This fact is intrinsically bound up with the revelation it has received. From the first moment, the God who speaks to Israel in the person of Abraham makes a promise: he promises a posterity, a nation, a land, a mysterious blessing which in some way includes every kind of good and will one day be poured out on all the nations. Later, in the days of slavery, God promises deliverance; in the time of exile, return and restoration. For Israel, to believe means to trust in the Word of God, in his faithfulness, his promises, it is to wait in confidence for their fulfilment. Gradually, with the experience of history and the preaching of the prophets, this hope fills out: what is expected is that God should put an end to the reign of ignorance, sin, pride, impiety and the evils which flow from them; that he should establish his Kingdom, a Kingdom of knowledge, justice, holiness, peace and happiness. To this very day, through all the diverse and changing representations of the coming and consummation of the Kingdom, this is the fundamental object of Israel's expectation: God made manifest, known, acknowledged, obeyed and served by all men, all nations. An ancient prayer, the *Alenu,* recited at the end of every synagogue service, well expresses the substance of this expectation:

> We therefore hope in thee, O Lord our God, that we may speedily behold the glory of thy might, when thou wilt remove the abominations from the earth, and the idols will be utterly cut off, when the world will be perfected under the kingdom of the Almighty, and all the children of flesh will call upon thy name, when thou wilt turn unto thyself all the wicked of the earth. Let all the inhabitants of the earth perceive and know that unto thee every knee must bow, every tongue must swear. Before thee, O Lord our God, let them bow and fall; and unto thy glorious name let them give honour; let them all accept the yoke of thy kingdom, and do thou reign over them speedily, and for ever and ever. For the kingdom is thine, and to all eternity thou wilt reign in glory; as it is written in thy Law, The Lord shall reign for ever and ever. And it is said, And the Lord shall be king over all the earth: in that day shall the Lord be One, and his name One.

The Election, the Covenant, the Torah with all its *mitzvot,* the whole mission of Israel as witness, as servant, as "kingdom of priests", are all wholly directed towards this end, this coming. This hope both embraces and reveals the real dimensions of Judaism, its historical and temporal dimension and its religious, theological dimension. These two together define the phenomenon of Judaism as a "mysticism in action", as a power acting entirely on the plane of history, yet wholly turned towards God, beyond history, and they help us to understand how religious and earthly values in Judaism are inextricably interwoven.

The expectation of the Messiah

God must reign first in Israel and then, through Israel, in the world. The idea of the kingdom of God in biblical tradition is inseparable from theocracy in Israel. The disappointments, the back-slidings, the historical misfortunes of the kingship in Israel brought the people of God increasingly to idealize the theocratic idea and its first faithful embodiment in David, the Lord's Anointed (*Meshiach,* whence Messiah; in Greek, *Christos*). The hope thus consisted in looking forward to the restoration of the theocracy, of the Kingdom of Israel, under the aegis of a new David, the Lord's Anointed *par excellence*, the Messiah. When God's people was deported and dispersed, its temple destroyed, this hope became also a hope for the return of the exiles, the ingathering of the dispersed and the rebuilding of the holy city and its temple, the restoration of its worship as well as of its kingdom. These are the main themes of Israel's Messianic hope, as they appear even in the biblical era, in the days of the great prophets, and as they were to be handed on, examined and elaborated in later Jewish tradition. As early as the biblical period, the Messianic theme inclined Jewish tradition to emphasize that element in its hopes which related specifically to the destiny of the people itself, the national element and also the particularist tendency, whereas the more general expectation of the Kingdom of God expressed rather the universalist tendency. As we have already observed, Jewish tradition has been divided between these two tendencies, one of which looks to see the people of Israel kept its place apart, its central rôle, its quasi-priestly function, even when the Messianic Kingdom is achieved, while the other holds that in the days of the Messiah the nations may well be incorporated into the fold of a single and universal people of God.

Out of all that ferment of Messianic ideas and movements, often strongly touched with national and political aspirations, which we find echoed in the apocalyptic literature and the New Testament itself, Pharisaic Judaism (which alone survived the disaster of A.D. 70) preserved and bequeathed to rabbinical Judaism only the religious and theological element. The destruction of the temple and the holy city—the exile of the *shechinah* itself, as later teachers of Israel said—helped to give the Messianic hope its full theological significance. Later on, the intense use made of the Messianic theme in Christian theology rather went to restrict its development in Jewish tradition. It was chiefly still later, when Judaism felt itself more settled and better protected in its relative isolation, and when at the same time its condition became specially difficult, that expectation became more ardent and Messianic speculation flourished again, periodically giving rise to the appearance of false Messiahs, even down to our own day.

One of the most significant attributes with which the discussions of the Rabbis and the meditations of the mystics have enriched the figure of the Messiah-King is his pre-existence. Before appearing to accomplish his mission, he pre-exists in the presence of God, like the Torah, the temple and other realities intimately related to God's designs. In other texts, however, before appearing in glory he is already present on earth, in obscurity and poverty. With the progress of the idea of redemptive suffering, the theme of a suffering Messiah became prominent also in the rabbinical and mystical theories of medieval Judaism. These speculations are often based on the poem of the "Suffering Servant" in Isaias 53. In order to resolve the problem raised by the Messianic interpretation of this text, an older tradition, dating from about the beginning of the Christian era, had taught that there would be two Messiahs: a Messiah, son of Joseph (or Ephraim), having to come and be put to death before the coming of the Messiah, son of David, who would bring about the Messianic restoration. On the other hand, the more rigorous discipline of medieval Jewish theology came to identify the suffering, humbled people of the Exile with the suffering Servant, and this idea has been widely adopted in modern Jewish thought. The actual coming of the Messiah and the victorious aspects of his work naturally occupy a considerable place in traditional literature: calculations of the date of the coming, the signs preceding it (the return of Elias, the Messianic "woes", etc.), descriptions of the glory and happiness of the Messianic Kingdom—which often verge on eschatological visions, combining the features of the restored earthly Jerusalem with those of the heavenly Jerusalem—views on the cosmic repercussions of the Messiah's work, etc.

But what matters more than this pictured content, with its many-coloured facets, is the actual nature of this hope. On the one hand it is the passive waiting for a miraculous divine intervention, a sovereign act of grace and faithfulness, which can only be prayed for with ardent supplication. On the other hand, as we have often seen, Israel's mission is to prepare and hasten the Messianic coming by its witness, its fidelity, its sufferings, by all the *mitzvot* performed every day by all its sons. These two aspects of the expectation are of the innermost essence of Judaism and are still vital in our day. In modern Judaism the tendency is certainly to lay less emphasis on the figure of the Messiah, and Liberal Judaism would perhaps almost sacrifice it altogether, in the hope of saving the substance of the traditional hope—not to mention some Liberals who would gladly reduce all Messianism to a vague hope in human progress. But in the life of the traditional Jew the daily observances continue to stimulate awareness of the active side of this hope, while the synagogue prayers constantly teach him to pray and watch for the sovereign initiative of the Lord. Here, for instance, is the tenth of the "Eighteen Blessings" recited every day:

> Sound the great horn for our freedom; lift up the ensign to gather our exiles, and gather us from the four corners of the earth. Blessed art thou, O Lord, who gatherest the banished ones of thy people, Israel. . . .
>
> And to Jerusalem, thy city, return in mercy, and dwell therein as thou hast spoken; rebuild it soon in our days as an everlasting building, and speedily set up therein the throne of David. Blessed art thou, O Lord, who rebuildest Jerusalem.
>
> Speedily cause the offspring of David, thy servant, to

flourish, and let his horn be exalted by thy salvation, because we wait for thy salvation all the day. Blessed art thou, O Lord, who causest the horn of salvation to flourish.

The world to come

On the question of man's individual destiny after death, we have space only for a brief sketch. In ancient rabbinical tradition, however, there is abundant material on the subject, in spite of this tradition's reluctance to speculate about the future life. But in medieval and modern Judaism these questions are generally little discussed. The underlying cause of this must no doubt be sought in the historical and corporate character of Judaism and in the dominance of the Messianic expectation in the expression of its hope.

But man's condition after death and the condition of mankind after the end of time are by no means outside the scope of Judaism's actual faith and hope. There is abundant and unequivocal evidence of the real teaching of traditional Jewish faith on the ultimate destinies of man: the importance for the "world to come" (*olam ha-bah*) of acts performed in "this world" (*olam ha-ze*), the reality of God's judgements and the eternal sanctions, the need to prepare for death, the need and efficacy of prayer for the dead, and finally the faith in the resurrection, so firmly held by the ancient Pharisees against the Sadducees (as we see in many passages of the Gospels and the Acts of the Apostles), and very often asserted in the synagogue prayers. All this is obviously part of the heritage of Jewish orthodoxy, though never clearly defined as forming part of it, except as regards the resurrection. These beliefs are in evident agreement with the Christian faith; they are simply rather less explicit on certain points. Besides the reasons we have mentioned, what has possibly prevented Judaism from defining them more closely is, on the one hand, a legitimate distrust of imaginative representations of heavenly truth and, on the other, a certain equally comprehensible unwillingness to express its faith in philosophical categories which are foreign to its tradition. In the Middle

Ages and even more in the modern world, Jewish thought has resorted more freely to these categories of thought and language, now the common property of all modern culture, but the real Jewish faith had not much to gain thereby.

The traditional expression of eschatological hopes, often mingled with features of the Messianic Kingdom and the "world to come", is perhaps all the richer and more suggestive for its obscurity and vagueness. There are points, too, on which the traditional terminology very aptly expresses the truths of the future life, for example, when it places the happiness of the just in the constant enjoyment of the *shechinah*, the presence of the glory of God. The *shechinah*, in fact, is a theme which is not only spiritually very rich and central in Jewish tradition but also one which best expresses the organic connection between the history of salvation and the final salvation itself, in the living faith and the theological hope of Israel.

CHAPTER V

WORSHIP AND PRAYER

RELIGIOUS RITES IN JEWISH LIFE

In the section on the observances of the Law, in the previous chapter, we emphasized that many of these *mitzvot* are directly concerned with worship. These actions, by means of which the community of Israel performs its fundamental duty, to be the "holy nation" vowed to God's service, can be divided into two main categories: the "service" of God in the strict sense—*avodah*—that is, the liturgical service in the synagogue or the home, and the other *mitzvot* to do with worship, which may be compared to the sacraments and sacramentals of the Church. This division does not imply any inequality in religious value, but simply a difference of subject-matter.

The liturgy properly so called, in synagogue or home, but always corporate, is essentially designed to sanctify *time*—seasons, weeks, days and hours—by the daily offices, the Sabbath, the festivals and fasts. The other religious observances, of a more personal nature, are intended to sanctify persons, actions, objects, etc. But naturally there are cases where this distinction is not very apparent. Before embarking on the liturgy in the strict sense, we shall rapidly review some of the more important of these religious observances.

Circumcision is a *mitzvah* of the highest order. It is through this that the newborn male child, on the eighth day after his birth, is incorporated into the stock of Abraham, the community of Israel, and participates in the Covenant and the divine promises. It is also by circumcision that the adult proselyte enters the community, but in this case circumcision is supplemented (and replaced, in the case of a woman) by a ritual bath. Circumcision is completed by a rite of initiation, consisting essentially in a first active and solemn participation in worship by the public reading of the Torah in the synagogue. At the age of thirteen this inaugurates the religious coming-of-age of the young Israelite and makes him an active member of the community, subject to all the commandments of the Torah, a *bar-mitzvah*, a "son of the commandment". This name is also given to the initiation ceremony itself.

Israel's character as a consecrated community is expressed in a mass of minute prescriptions concerning dwelling-places, clothing, diet, ritual purity, etc. In connection with the sanctification of the house we may note the practice of fixing to the door-posts a little tubular case (*mezuzah*), containing a piece of parchment with the text of the *Shema* ("Hear, O Israel"), the proclamation of the unity of God. As to clothing, present practice chiefly concerns the dress for prayer, the wearing (obligatory at some services) of the prayer-shawl called the *tallit*, fitted with four fringes (*tzitzit*), and of the "phylacteries" (*tephillin*), cases which likewise contain the *Shema*, with some other biblical verses, and are fixed on the forehead and the left arm. More complicated are the dietary laws prescribing a ritual food, or *kasher*, but here we can only give some of its main principles. It is forbidden to consume the blood (and hence there is a special, ritual method of slaughtering animals), to consume the flesh of animals reckoned unclean (such as the pig), or to mix milk foods and flesh at the same meal, etc. The meaning of these prescriptions is not easy to grasp, but to the pious Jew this does not in the least diminish their value as a *mitzvah*, a performance of the Law of God and a hallowing of his name. It is the same with the laws about ritual purity of the body and the rites of purification, but their symbolic meaning is more obvious and they have played a considerable part in the organization of Jewish life and the formation of traditional Jewish customs.

On the other hand, the significance of those very characteristic *mitzvot*, the Blessings, is perfectly clear and often very rich. By these short prayer-forms of blessing, thanksgiving and praise, all the actions, objects and circumstances of life are expressly related to God and consecrated to him. This practice clearly illustrates the religious ideal of Judaism, which assumes that daily life and religion are completely interwoven.

THE LITURGY OF THE SYNAGOGUE

The strictly liturgical acts of Jewish life take place either in the synagogue or in the home. The most important occasions of the domestic liturgy will be noted in the next section, under "holy days". The present section deals only with the synagogue liturgy and its general features.

In the historical sketch in Chapter II, there was some mention of the origins of the institution of the synagogue, its development after the Exile and in the Dispersion, and the vital importance of these places of meeting, study and prayer. When the Temple disappeared in the disaster of the year 70, the synagogue was ready to take over its rôle in the liturgical life of Judaism. The structure of its services—composed of readings, prayers and preaching—was already formed, with the nucleus of its basic prayers. The building itself was henceforth centred on what is the heart of the synagogue worship, the chest or "holy ark" containing the precious scrolls of the Torah, and on the platform which is used for the readings and the recitation of certain prayers. It is usual, though not obligatory, for the service to be presided over by the rabbi, the teacher commissioned to instruct and preach, and to be led by the officiating minister (*chazzan*), but neither has any priestly character.[1] The synagogue liturgy preserves only one trace of the ancient priesthood: the blessing at the end of the

[1] Even the *semichah*, the ancient rabbinical ordination, which disappeared with the decline of Palestinian Judaism, only conferred a teaching and judicial authority.

office, which is reserved to descendants of the priestly class (*ha-Kohanim*). But while no priestly functions remain, the presence of a "number" or quorum (*minyan*), of ten religiously adult men, is a compulsory condition for the performance of any act of public worship, whether in the synagogue or outside the synagogue services, and for all devotional *mitzvot* of a public character.

The general structure of the synagogue services is based on two centres: the *Shema*, which is Israel's *Credo*, and the reading of the Torah. To these two was very soon added a third vital part, the prayer called the Eighteen Blessings or *Shemoneh-Esreh* (the number being actually variable and usually reaching nineteen), also called the *Amidah* (because recited standing), or simply *Tephillah*, Prayer, the prayer *par excellence*.

The reading of the Torah, the whole Pentateuch, is divided into *sidrot*, fixed lessons, for all the Sabbaths of the year, the festivals having their own proper lessons. This arrangement of the lessons springs from the Babylonian tradition, for its annual cycle supplanted the triennial cycle formerly practised in the Palestinian communities. To the *sidrot* of the Torah is added, for every Sabbath or festival, a selected *haphtorah*, a lesson taken from the other books of the Bible, usually from the Prophets.

These lessons, especially those of the Torah, are framed in a collection of prayers and blessings, of almost entirely biblical inspiration, mostly designed to magnify the Torah and thank the Lord for the gift of the Torah. The same is true of the prayers and blessings enshrining the solemn liturgical recitation of the *Shema*, as is natural when we remember that to Jewish tradition this represents the quintessence, as it were, of the Torah. As for the prayer of the Eighteen Blessings—already quoted in Chapter IV—by the fullness and richness of its content it has become the gem of the synagogue services. Under the form of blessing, praise and prayer, it includes, in fact, all the great themes of Israel's faith and aspirations. Another important prayer, besides the *Alenu*, the closing prayer already mentioned, is the *Kaddish*, a beautiful Aramaic prayer for the hallowing of the Lord's name and the coming of his kingdom, which is recited between the different parts of the office, and has generally been used, since the Middle Ages, as a prayer for the dead. The *Kaddish* has often been compared with the Lord's Prayer, and there is indeed a marked similarity between the two prayers.

Besides some psalm verses recited in the liturgical forms, certain psalms recited in full occupy an important place in the offices, as well as hymns and various liturgical poems, called *piyyutim*. These insertions are sometimes of rather late date and comparatively few of them are preserved in the present liturgy, but they are drawn from a very rich vein of liturgical poetry, which from the Middle Ages down to modern times has been a kind of translation of the themes of midrashic literature.

The synagogue prayers are arranged in three daily obligatory offices: the morning office (*schacharit*), which is the most elaborate, and on Sabbaths and festivals is enlarged by a "supplementary" office, the *musaph*; the afternoon office (*minchah*) and the evening office (*maariv*).

After a long evolution, the texts of the synagogue liturgy have been collected in two kinds of liturgical books or Rituals: the *Siddur*, containing the daily prayers, and the *Machzor*, whose different volumes contain the offices of the different festivals of the year. Besides these two basic rituals, there are other liturgical books, like the compilations of the *Selichot* or prayers of penitence for the days of fasting or mourning, and the *Haggadah*, used for the domestic celebration of the Passover.

As we mentioned in Chapter II, modern Judaism comprises several rites or *minhagim*, especially two main groups of rites: the *Ashkenazi* or German group, and the *Sephardi* or Spanish-Portuguese group; but there also exist other groups, both within and without these two. The origin of this division of rites goes back to the differences between the liturgical uses of Palestinian and Babylonian Judaism in the golden days of the formation of post-biblical tradition. But as these rites all retain the same liturgical language (Hebrew), the same basic prayers and the same structure in their offices, the differences between them are only secondary, and certainly much less important than those between the different rites in the Catholic Church or in the non-Roman Eastern Churches.

In the first period of the liturgy's formation, the content of the not strictly biblical prayers formed part of an oral tradition and allowed much room for freedom and variety. This was the case with the whole tradition, and we find it equally in the history of the formation of the Christian liturgies. It was only gradually that the texts were committed to writing, in forms which thereafter remained fixed. These texts, which alternate in the liturgy with entirely biblical texts, are often composed mainly of biblical verses, expressions and echoes. When they go beyond the scriptural element they usually draw on tradition, especially the midrashic. This means that the themes, the tone, the language and inspiration of these prayers are always fundamentally biblical. They are an even better proof of how deeply Judaism is rooted in the Bible than the rabbinical tradition which, though continually dealing with the Torah, necessarily adds to it or departs from it to a greater extent. But we should be wrong to suppose that the liturgy has remained untouched by the different spiritual movements which Judaism has produced in the course of its post-biblical history. Thus the determining influence of the Cabbalah on almost all Judaism at the end of the Middle Ages has left its mark in the introduction of various prayers of Cabbalistic inspiration. Some of these prayers were eliminated during the attempts at purgation undertaken during the nineteenth century, but others keep their place in the synagogue offices.[2]

[2] We shall not enlarge on other recent bypaths of Jewish liturgy, as they do not concern the traditional liturgy, which is the subject of this chapter. For of course, as there now exist Orthodox, Conservative and Reformed communities, one may equally speak of Orthodox, Conservative or Reformed liturgies.

Finally we must emphasize an essentially twofold aspect of Jewish liturgy. On the one hand it is historical, precisely because it is biblical, because all its content is drawn from the manifestation of the Lord *in* the history of his people. On the other hand, its tendency is to make that history *present*, for this is the constant and habitual attitude of Jewish biblical interpretation and of all traditional *midrash*. When, in the synagogue or at home, the faithful Jew takes part in the festivals and prayers of the assembly of Israel, he takes part, in a way, in the inauguration of the Covenant and the great stages in the history of the people of God. This explains the immense place in Jewish piety held by the liturgy. Here too we find a striking relationship with the liturgy of the Church, which also, by its character as a mystery and its sacramental nature, tends to renew, to make present, the great moments of the history of salvation and to enable the faithful to take their part in them.

In addition to this profound analogy, we could point out many links of dependence and relationship between the Jewish and Christian liturgies, but their study, difficult in any case, would exceed the limits of these pages. The mere mention of these connections may remind us that the oldest basic elements of the liturgical heritage of modern Judaism are the very same as were known and practised in the synagogues of their time by our Lord, his disciples and the earliest Christian generations.

THE "HOLY DAYS" OF THE JEWISH YEAR

The framework of the liturgy is provided by the Jewish calendar, based on the lunar year of twelve months, to which is added a supplementary thirteenth month every two or three years. The religious year begins in principle with the month of *Nisan*, the month of the Passover, in spring, and ends with the month of *Adar*. But in fact the civil year, which begins with *Tishri*, the seventh month of the religious year, has largely prevailed, so that the religious festival of the New Year itself is celebrated on the first day of *Tishri*. The new moons are celebrated in the framework of the daily offices. The cycle of liturgical reading of the Torah, mentioned in the last section, does not coincide with the calendar year. This cycle is so calculated as to end on the 23rd day of *Tishri*, the octave of *Succoth* (the festival of Tabernacles; see below), and Festival of the Torah, after which, on the next Sabbath, the new cycle begins again.

In one sense, among all the *moadim* or solemn days which mark the Jewish year, none excels the Sabbath in its importance and profound influence on Jewish life. We are familiar with the texts of the Pentateuch and the Prophets in which the Sabbath rest is justified, imposed, detailed and praised. As early as post-exilic Judaism the Sabbath appears as a fundamental institution, and its function is of the highest importance in all rabbinical literature.

As a holy day and a day of rest from the beginning, the Sabbath has a twofold aspect, religious, and human or social. Hence the need for exact regulation of the Sabbath rest; this began in the biblical period, was perfected by constant endeavour in all rabbinical tradition and has been faithfully and meticulously observed by pious Jews down to this day, from nightfall on Friday evening till Saturday evening, following the method by which the liturgical day is reckoned in Judaism. The communal aspect of the Sabbath rest is obvious, and its observance can be very difficult outside traditional communities. But the scrupulous observance of the Sabbath rest has a religious value of the first order and holds a prominent place among the *mitzvot*. For consecrating the day entirely to God and making it what it ought to be, a "Sabbath of the Lord", it is as essential as participation in the liturgical offices.

But the purely external observance of the Sabbath rest would be useless if the time thus withdrawn from the weekly work were not devoted to prayer and the study of the Law. For the community of Israel, it is above all by the Sabbath that time and life must be consecrated. That is what makes it the holy day above all others, the day of the Lord and his praise. For all these reasons the Sabbath, for the faithful Jew, is also supremely a day of joy. Its weekly celebration has impressed a profound mark on the synagogue worship as well as on worship in the home. Of the latter, indeed, it is both the peak and the continuous pattern. Apart from the actual rest and the services and the hours devoted to study and reading, it involves a whole family ritual: the lighting of the Sabbath lamp by the mistress of the house at the Sabbath's opening, the blessing given by the father of the family to his children, the reading of the eulogy of the "valiant woman", the blessing of the Sabbath cup of wine (the *Kiddush*), followed by the solemn meal. All this takes place in festal array and in an atmosphere of infectious joy (*oneg-shabbat*: the joy of the Sabbath), which possesses traditional Jewish families on Friday evening, when the Sabbath is welcomed with a mystical, poetical gaiety, like a betrothed or a queen, till the hour when they bid it farewell on Saturday evening, with the return of the concluding office.

The other holy days, the festivals and fasts of the Jewish year, can be divided into four groups:

1. The three ancient festivals of pilgrimage (to the Temple at Jerusalem): Passover (*Pesach*), Pentecost (*Shavuot*) and Tabernacles (*Succoth*), the last being followed by the Festival of the Closing (*Shemini atzeret*) and the Festival of the Law (*Simchat Torah*).

2. The two "awe-inspiring days" (*yamim moraim*), or austere festivals: the New Year (*Rosh ha-Shanah*) and the Day of Atonement (*Yom Kippur*), also called the Day of the Great Pardon.

The festivals belonging to these two groups are all of biblical origin and perpetuate the liturgical tradition of the Second Temple, though in the transfer from Temple to synagogue their celebration has had to be modified. The holy days of the two following groups, however, are of rabbinical origin:

3. Two festivals of joyful, popular commemoration, *Chanuccah* or the Dedication, also called the Feast of Lights, and *Purim*, the Day of the Lots.

4. Various days of commemoration, especially the four days of fasting (*taanit*), in memory of various sad events in Israel's past. The most important of these fast-days is the Ninth of Av (*Tisha be-Av*), a day of mourning in memory of the destruction of the First Temple by Nabuchodonosor and of the Second Temple by Titus.

We cannot here enter into the details of the liturgy of these different festivals, but will simply give some notes on the spirit, meaning and liturgical characteristics of those belonging to the first three of these categories.

Passover or *Pesach* (passing) begins on the 15th of *Nisan* and is celebrated for eight days. Commemorating the Exodus from Egypt, the great deliverance which marks the birth of Israel as a nation and is the pledge and foreshadowing of the great messianic deliverance, Passover is the greatest festival of the Jewish year, both in its theological meaning and also in popular sentiment. It is also called the Festival of the Azymes or the Unleavened Bread, one of its features being the exclusive use of this bread, in memory of the going out from Egypt (cf. Exod. 23). Nowadays the Passover preserves very little trace of the agricultural character it originally had, together with its religious significance. The Passover liturgy is marked chiefly by the reading of the Song of Songs, applied to Israel in its relations with God, since its deliverance and through all its history. The first part of what formed the centre of the ancient celebration of the Passover, namely, the sacrifice of the lamb, having ceased with the Temple, there remains only the second part to form the centre of the modern Passover celebration; it is the Paschal meal, the *Seder*, celebrated in the family circle on the eve of the first day of the feast, and sometimes also of the second. It follows the biblical rite, but is supplemented by later elements drawn from rabbinical tradition or from folklore. The symbolic rites (with the roasted bone representing the lamb, the unleavened loaves and the bitter herbs) performed and presided over by the father of the family before the meal, are enshrined in the narrative of the Exodus from Egypt, the *Haggadah* of the

Pesach. The family nature of the *Seder* is emphasized by the part entrusted to the children, and especially to the youngest child, in the recitation of the events of the Exodus according to the *Haggadah.* These rites are followed by the solemn meal, dominated by the joy of the deliverance, the whole concluding with the singing of the great *Hallel,* composed of psalms of thanksgiving.

The festival of Weeks or *Shavuot,* which falls seven weeks after the Passover (whence the name "Pentecost" or fiftieth day), preserves more of its original agricultural meaning: it is the feast of the harvest and the firstfruits, for which the reading of the Book of Ruth is singularly appropriate. Primitive rabbinical tradition gave it a new meaning, without suppressing the old: that of a commemoration or even an anniversary of the giving of the Torah, of its promulgation on Sinai (whence the reading of the Decalogue in the morning office). The liturgical period called the *Omer,* between Passover and the Festival of Weeks, has a certain note of austerity. The historical meaning given to *Shavuot* by tradition in fact makes this period a memorial of the sojourn of the Hebrews in the wilderness between leaving Egypt and reaching Sinai.

Succoth, the festival of Tabernacles or Booths, falls in autumn, as it comes some days after the "awe-inspiring days" of the New Year and the Great Pardon, brings with it new rejoicings and thanksgivings for the Lord's blessings and especially, at this season, for all the fruits of the earth. But it is above all a joyful remembrance of the Lord's watchful protection during the Hebrews' wandering in the wilderness, when they lived in tents. Following the command of Lev. 23. 39–43, for seven days all dwell in booths of foliage; they sing the thanksgiving psalms of the *Hallel,* waving branches of the tree called *lulav* (palm) and the *etrog* (citron), for the blessing of the feast and for the *Hoshannah* of the daily procession, which is kept with special solemnity on the last day of the festival.

Rosh ha-Shanah, the day of the New Year, is of a somewhat different character. Its importance in Jewish life is considerable. In spite of its biblical origin (Lev. 23. 23–5), its significance and its liturgy are derived in essence from the synagogue tradition. The home takes a much smaller part in its celebration than on the three feasts of pilgrimage. As on the day of the Great Pardon, the celebration is wholly centred on the synagogue offices, which are also much more complicated for these two austere days than for the three we have mentioned, and contain many more elements peculiar to them. Their tone is generally solemn, insistently recalling the Majesty of God, his sovereign decrees and just judgements which determine man's destiny. For that destiny, says tradition, the New Year is of decisive importance: on that day God judges the deeds of the past year and disposes the events of the year to come. It is therefore the time to repent, to implore pardon for the past, divine help for the future, by pleading God's past favours. The litanical prayer "Our Father, our King!", appointed for *Rosh ha-Shanah* and *Yom Kippur* and the ten days between them, vividly expresses these sentiments. But it is not only their own personal lot which concerns the faithful, it is the fate of the whole people. So we also find expressed there an ardent longing for the ingathering of Israel, just as, for example, in the Passover liturgy. The blare of the *shophar*, the trumpet of ram's horn, which is sounded to recall both the trumpet-blasts of Sinai and those of the Day of Judgement, adds its contribution to the atmosphere proper to this solemn day.

Yom Kippur, the Day of Atonement, holds a unique place in the Jewish liturgy—of which it is the culminating point—and in all Jewish spirituality. It is a day of *teshuvah* (return), of penitence, atonement, purification for the individual, but above all for the people, for it is all Israel which has sinned, has transgressed the Torah, has broken the Covenant, and in this sin all its members are corporately involved. Appointed for the 10th of *Tishri*, the Great Pardon follows the remembrance of the Lord's judgements and decrees on the New Year. The solemnity and strict obligation of this day of penitence are trenchantly inculcated in Scripture itself (Lev. 16

and 23. 26–32). The burnt-offerings, the entry of the high priest into the Holy of Holies, the driving out of the scape-goat, symbolically charged with the sins of the people; all that came to an end with the destruction of the Temple. Their solemn liturgical remembrance—the *seder avodah*—is central in the liturgy of the Great Pardon. There still remain, at present, the strict fast of twenty-four hours and the five offices which fill almost the whole day. To take the place of the vanished expiatory sacrifices, tradition has obviously sought, on this day, to multiply prayers for divine pardon. To the four festival offices it has here added a fifth, the office of Conclusion. The great solemn confession of past sins, which is the highlight of the liturgy of the *Kippur*, is repeated at each of these offices after the *Tephillah*. These liturgical confessions urge the whole community and each of its members to repentance and spiritual renewal, calling on them to make reparation for their sins, to be reconciled and to forgive offences. At the same time, fervent prayer is made for divine pardon and the purification of the people, which must hasten the restoration and the rebuilding of the Temple, and God's protection is sought against evil. The appeals to God's faithfulness and mercy on this day are specially urgent and solemn. And yet, in spite of the atmosphere of affliction and fear, arising from awareness of the gravity of the sins committed, the joyful note of trust, of the certainty of the divine mercy and pardon, and the spirit of adoration, praise and thanksgiving, are constantly present in the liturgy of *Yom Kippur*. The very deep hold of this day and its liturgy over the Jewish soul is of course obvious in those who take part in it with fervour, but it is surprisingly apparent even in those who have strayed far from tradition.

We conclude this chapter with a brief glance at two secondary but characteristic festivals of the Jewish year, alike in that they commemorate biblical events but, as festivals, are of post-biblical origin, alike also in that they have a joyful, popular character, more domestic than of the synagogue, and that they are not holidays from work. The first, the Dedication

—*Chanuccah*—or the Feast of Lights, is celebrated for eight days from the 25th of *Kislev*, which places it about Christmas. It commemorates the purification and rededication of the Temple after its profanation by the heathen, under Judas Maccabaeus, and at the same time the victories of the Machabees and the deliverance of Israel from Syrian rule. As a sign of rejoicing and in memory of the relighting of the sanctuary lamp, the eight candles of the *menorah* (a candelabrum of eight branches) are successively kindled on the eight days of the feast. The feast of *Purim,* on the 14th of *Adar*, is still more marked by popular rejoicings and by folklore. It is kept in memory of Esther who, with the help of Mardochaeus, saved Israel from the wicked Aman's plot of extermination, in the days of Assuerus. At the centre of the liturgy of this feast we naturally find the reading of the Book of Esther, one of the five small scrolls, the *megillot*.

These "holy days", all so different—which is one of the reasons we have dealt with them at some length—have played and still play a vital rôle in handing down the tradition of Judaism, in developing its spirituality and in maintaining all that solid and complex human reality which is Jewish life.

CHAPTER VI

MYSTICAL TRENDS IN JUDAISM

The historical sketch in Chapter II and the doctrinal exposition in Chapter IV dealt, in essentials, with the most classical line of the tradition of rabbinical Judaism. But our picture of Judaism would really be too poor and incomplete without some pages on the main complementary trends and the most marked mystical tendencies in Judaism. In many cases we find that the origin of these trends lies in a reaction against elements in the talmudic or rabbinical tradition which might be one-sided, from the doctrinal, legal or spiritual point of view. Some of these movements resulted in the formation of actual sects, separated from the main body of traditional Judaism and deemed by it to be heterodox. Others, on the contrary, though at first they aroused very keen controversy and for long remained the object of hostility on the part of the rabbinical authorities, were able in the end to maintain themselves in the framework of orthodox tradition or to be restored to it, and so, by their special contribution and influence, to affect the traditional teaching, prayer and institutions. A typical example of the former sort, the sects, is provided by *Karaism*, a movement which began in the eighth century in Babylonia, under the dominant influence of Anan ben David. Connected with the tradition of the Sadducees, the *Karaites* ("Scripturals") rejected the authority of the oral Law and the rabbinical tradition and advocated a return to the letter of Scripture, to Scripture alone. They encountered violent opposition from the representatives of rabbinism, but were able to organize themselves, to increase, to display considerable religious and intellectual activity, and to exert great influence. But from the thirteenth century the Karaite schism began to decline. Today there remain only a small number of followers, with no great vitality of a strictly Karaite nature. Some comparatively recent Messianic movements, actuated by a quite different inspiration, especially by the influence of the Cabbalah, for a time enjoyed a dazzling but ephemeral success, only to fall back into the condition of small sects, surviving in a semi-clandestine state, as happened to the *Sabbatianism* of the seventeenth century and the *Frankism* of the eighteenth.

What concerns us here is not the history of these movements but what remains of them, whether as an integral contribution to the heritage of Judaism, or as a particular current of thought and spirituality within traditional Judaism. If we here speak of *mystical* tendencies, the term must not be taken in a too strict technical or theological sense. It will simply be used to denote, on the one hand, a fervent interior piety, in love with the Absolute, and at the same time aspiring to great intimacy with God, in an atmosphere of great inward liberty, and expressing itself in a style more lyrical than juridical or intellectual; in short, a piety of the type we shall find in *Chasidism.* On the other hand, by the same term of "mystical" or "mysticism" we denote movements which are centred less on the love than on the knowledge of God, a knowledge which is mysterious, even hidden, directed to a sort of contemplative *gnosis,* of which we find examples in the various *Cabbalistic* currents. But to appreciate the true place of these trends in Judaism as a whole we must not forget that similar aspirations appear often enough in the most classical tradition of Jewish spirituality, and in the Bible itself.

The mystical richness of Israel's biblical heritage needs no demonstration, any more than the profoundly interior piety reflected in many of the Psalms, the spiritual food of the "poor men of Yahweh" and of countless generations of faithful Israelites after them. The living faith of Judaism and its ardent quest for understanding of God's Word have in them a constant mystical vein, even if it is sometimes masked by the practical and legal *style* of the religion of the Torah. No doubt this mystical vein often seeks means of expression and conditions of expansion which are marginal to rabbinical tradition, but it can equally be expressed in works of spirituality which, while using certain resources drawn from Christian or Moslem spirituality, or even from Greek thought, are still in the most authentic line of the tradition of the Bible, the Midrash and the synagogue liturgy. An outstanding example of this is the greatest classic of Jewish spirituality, the *Introduction to the duties of hearts,* by Bahya ibn Paquda (in Spain, eleventh century), which is a genuine manual of the interior life and asceticism, wholly directed to the pure love of God and a perfectly orthodox reaction to the excesses of legalism. The wide circulation of such a book in the past and the present is enough to prove that true mysticism is not just on the fringes but in the very heart of Jewish tradition.

The Cabbalah

Rightly or wrongly, when one speaks of Jewish mysticism, one generally thinks chiefly of the Cabbalah. This word (which means "tradition") stands for a very vast and complex body of traditions and ideas, whose origins, somewhat obscure in part, are connected with various writings and esoteric streams of gnosis, speculative mysticism, theosophy, cosmogony, etc. The formation of this complex of ideas was spread over about the same period as that of Pharisaic and rabbinical Judaism, and there were many reciprocal influences and exchanges between the two. Later on, in medieval Spain, the still confused body of Cabbalistic traditions was strongly marked by Jewish-Arab philosophical and theological speculation, which enabled it to acquire a firmer philosophical structure and to systematize its doctrines. Thus, between the thirteenth and the sixteenth centuries, there appeared the great Cabbalistic systems, that of Abulafia, that of the *Zohar* ("The Book of Splendours"), the most classical work of the Cabbalah, and that of Luria, whose Cabbalistic theology has perhaps exercised the strongest influence on modern Judaism. The disaster which overtook Spanish Judaism at the end of the Middle Ages had the effect, for Cabbalistic centres, of a great expansion and a great renewal of fervour. It was above all from the seventeenth century that the Cabbalistic element began to spread more widely among both Ashkenazi and Sephardi communities, in rabbinical speculation, in the liturgy, etc. It is the presence of this Cabbalistic element in the various modern manifestations of Jewish life and thought that constitutes one of the *raisons d'être* of this chapter.

What, then, is the characteristic attitude of this Cabbalism, so omnipresent and so indefinable? The Cabbalist Jew, like the non-Cabbalist, takes his stand within the tradition of Judaism, but he seeks to interpret it all in the light of the esoteric traditions of the Cabbalah, with its own methods and symbolism. Thus, besides the more theological or metaphysical aspects of Cabbalistic speculation, the interpretation of the destiny, the mission and the sufferings of Israel holds a very important place in Cabbalistic thought, and there is no doubt that this is one of the points in which the influence of the Cabbalah on modern Jewish thought and literature has been most felt. Fairly often, too, Cabbalistic elements are mingled with the interpretation of the biblical stories of creation, of Paradise and of sin, as with speculations on the attributes of God, the problem of evil, etc. But on the whole, to be fair, Jewish tradition has offered a firm resistance to the penetration of Gnostic or dualist elements.

Properly Cabbalistic centres hold a comparatively small place in the modern Jewish world, and wholly Cabbalistic elements integrated into the common tradition of Judaism are very limited: But between the two one may detect "Cabbalizing" tendencies or influences in many Jewish religious centres which are reckoned among the most active and fervent. In conclusion we may point out, in this connection, a great revival of interest in studies on the Cabbalah, which among other things has made possible a better assessment of the importance of Cabbalistic influences, not only in Jewish life, but also in the history of Christian thought and in modern philosophy.

Chasidism

Like the Cabbalah, Chasidism is complementary to the rabbinical tradition, providing it with a valuable counterpoise. Though at first it met with violent opposition, it has succeeded in maintaining itself, guarding its own heritage and in turn exerting a profound influence on all Jewish communities. Unlike the Cabbalah, it has been able to expand widely and to touch the great masses of Ashkenazi Judaism.

There is no historical connection between this Chasidism and the Chasidism of the Rhineland which flourished in the twelfth century, although the name (from *chasid*, pious or devout) covers certain analogies between the two movements. The earlier Chasidism was a popular movement of piety, ascetical, mystical, even ecstatic, sometimes bordering on pantheistic mysticism. It played an important part in the history of Jewish piety, but had no *direct* continuation or descendants, and today nothing remains of it but its writings. Its essential legacy, the *Sepher Chasidim*, is one of the great monuments of Jewish spirituality.

The modern Chasidic movement springs from the teaching and example of Baal Shem Tov, who lived in the Carpathians in the eighteenth century. There can be no doubt that this simple, humble, affective devotion satisfied a deep longing; so joyful, close to nature, contemplative but not speculative, free of all legalistic stiffness and steeped in the best mystical heritage of the Cabbalah, but innocent of its speculative, gnostic and esoteric side. In spite of the distrust and opposition of the rabbinical authorities, the new devotion rose like a tidal wave, and in a surprisingly short time had won over innumerable traditional communities of eastern Europe, arousing in them extraordinary enthusiasm, fervour and spiritual revival. It also produced an organized movement, looking to the day when it could be fully integrated into rabbinical orthodoxy, when opposition should have ceased.

The ideal *chasid* is a Jew whose whole life is steeped in piety, whose observances and obedience to the Law are all inspired by love and overflowing in joy. The *kavannah*, the religious intention governing all his activity so as to make it an *avodah*, a service of God, is the fruit of interior concentration and asceticism and of a contemplative attitude resting on the intimate presence of God. At the height of the true *devekut*, or unitive devotion, there is ecstasy. To reach it, certain Chasidim aspire to an ecstatic type of prayer, employing to this end even physical means, such as rhythmic movements.

One of the movement's most original and characteristic aspects has been the rôle of the *tzaddikim* (the Just), spiritual guides and community leaders, surrounded with extraordinary popular veneration, to whom the people attributed unrivalled spiritual authority, mediatorial functions and miraculous powers. The legends and teachings of the celebrated *tzaddikim* form the groundwork of the vast popular and didactic literature to which the Chasidic movement has given birth. In spite of some debased elements of folklore and the superstitions which have crept into them, Chasidism has produced undeniable spiritual fruits and has effectively contributed to a definite revival and deepening of traditional Ashkenazi Judaism.

At the present day, in America and Israel (and to some extent also in Europe), the Chasidic communities preserve their own recognizable ways and sometimes even their own organizations, while still remaining in the very heart of orthodoxy. But outside it too, for example in the communities of the Reform, and even beyond the borders of Judaism,

Chasidic spirituality has met with much sympathy and has been able to exert a certain influence. Nobody now denies that genuine Chasidism represents an authentic component of Jewish tradition and that without it modern Judaism would present a very different appearance.

CONCLUSION

Some of our readers may feel that the picture of Judaism we have so rapidly sketched is too beautiful, too idealized, too little in accordance with their accepted ideas or personal experience. But even if personal experience is real, profound and sufficiently extensive—which is not always the case—what can it prove? At the most, that as individuals the Jews are men like everyone else, that it is as hard for them to achieve their religion's ideas as it is for us, that they respond to their vocation no more easily than we do. Would we wish our faith and our Church to be judged by chance encounters, in the lives of those who bear the name of Christian? And if not, why use two sets of weights and measures?

As to the often very confused image which has been printed on our conscious and even subconscious minds by accepted ideas, that is, by countless imperceptible influences, what is it worth? Is it not too often a distorted image, in fact a tendentious caricature, at once the hardened fruit and the still living seed of an ancient legacy of ignorance, resentment and contempt?

If we are to recognize the face of a brother, we need a brother's eyes. We have tried to look at the face of Judaism, not through the spectacles of any passion or illusion, but simply with the eyes of a brother. No doubt this requires an effort of sincerity, of understanding, or respect in our study of the features of this faraway brother, this elder brother who has suffered so much and, in spite of everything, has been faithful to his share of the heritage. We need above all to be clearly aware of our own roots, and of the solidarity of both our destinies, still surviving through all the separations, the conflicts and the vicissitudes of history. We must always be conscious that we all belong to the same family, the family of the people of God, and be certain that in God's designs that family is essentially one.

The Christian cannot be really objective in his study of the face of his Jewish brother if he does not set himself to look first for the family features, for the marks of our common roots, our common heritage and our common hope.

GLOSSARY OF HEBREW WORDS

Cabbalah: literally: "tradition". In mystical sense, see Chapter VI.
Chasidim: the pious. See Chapter VI.
chesed: grace.
haggadah: teaching by stories, parables, etc.
halachah: authoritative teaching; walk, step, law.
kavannah: religious intention, devotion.
midrash: interpretation; finding new meanings in Scripture.
Mishnah: repetition; codifications containing the core of the Oral Law.
mitzvah: commandment; fulfilment of the commandment; good work.
shechinah: the presence of God's glory.
Talmud: teaching. See Chapter II.
tannaim: repeaters; teachers of first two Christian centuries.
Targum: paraphrase; Aramaic interpretations of the Bible.
tephillah: prayer.
teshuvah: repentance.
Torah: (1) the Pentateuch; (2) the written and oral Law, including all talmudic teaching.
tzaddik: just; holy; see also Chapter VI.
Yeshivot: traditional talmudic schools.

SELECT BIBLIOGRAPHY

In this series: GÉLIN, Albert: *The Religion of Israel.*

Reference works

ROTH, C. (Editor): *The Standard Jewish Encyclopaedia*, Jerusalem and Tel Aviv, Massadah Publishing Co., 1958–9.

RUNES, D. (Editor): *Concise Dictionary of Judaism*, London, Peter Owen, and New York, Philosophical Library, 1959.

SINGER, I. (Editor): *The Jewish Encyclopaedia*, 12 volumes, New York, Funk and Wagnalls, 1901–6.

ZAEHNER, R. C. (Editor): *Concise Encyclopaedia of Living Faiths*, London, Hutchinson, and New York, Hawthorn, 1959.

ABRAHAMS, L. (Editor): *The Legacy of Israel*, London and New York, Oxford Univ. Press, 1927.

AGAR, Herbert: *The Saving Remnant*, London, Hart Davis, 1961.

BARON, S. W.: *Social and Religious History of the Jews*, New York, Columbia Univ. Press, 1957.

BELKIN, S.: *In His Image*, London and New York, Abelard-Schumann, 1961.

BERNSTEIN, Philip: *What the Jews Believe*, London, Allen and Unwin, and New York, Farrar Strauss, 1960.

BIRNBAUM, P.: *Daily Prayer Book*, New York, Hebrew Publishing Co., n.d.

COHEN, A.: *Everyman's Talmud*, London, Dent, 1932, and New York, Dutton, revised edn 1954.

DANIEL-ROPS: *Israel and the Ancient World*, London, Eyre and Spottiswoode, and New York, Longmans, 1949.

EPSTEIN, I.: *Judaism*, Harmondsworth and Baltimore, Penguin, 1959.

FINKELSTEIN, L.: *The Pharisees*, Philadelphia, Jewish Publications, 1938.

RICCIOTTI, G.: *History of Israel*, Milwaukee, Bruce, 1955.

SCHOLEM, G.: *Major Trends in Jewish Mysticism*, London, Thames and Hudson, and New York, Schocken, 1955.

USSHER, A.: *The Magic People*, London, Gollancz, and New York, Devin-Adair, 1950.

The Twentieth Century Encyclopedia of Catholicism

The number of each volume indicates its place in the over-all series and not the order of publication.

PART ONE: KNOWLEDGE AND FAITH

1. What Does Man Know?
2. Is Theology a Science?
3. The Meaning of Tradition
4. The Foundations of Faith
5. Do Dogmas Change?
6. What is Faith?
7. God's Word to Man
8. Myth or Mystery?
9. What is a Miracle?
10. Is There a Christian Philosophy?
11. Early Christian Philosophy
12. Medieval Christian Philosophy
13. The Basis of Belief
14. Does Christianity Oppose Science?
15. The God of Reason

PART TWO: THE BASIC TRUTHS

16. The Worship of God
17. What is the Trinity?
18. The Holy Spirit
19. In the Hands of the Creator
20. The Problem of Evil
21. Who is the Devil?
22. Freedom and Providence
23. The Theology of Grace
24. The Incarnation
25. What is Redemption?
26. The Communion of Saints
27. Faith, Hope and Charity
28. Life After Death

PART THREE: THE NATURE OF MAN

29. The Origins of Man
30. Evolution
31. What is Man?
32. What is Life?
33. What is Psychology?
34. Man in His Environment
35. Man and Metaphysics
36. Psychical Phenomena

PART FOUR: THE MEANS OF REDEMPTION

37. Prayer
38. The Nature of Mysticism
39. Spiritual Writers of the Early Church
40. Spiritual Writers of the Middle Ages
41. Post-Reformation Spirituality
42. Spirituality in Modern Times
43. What are Indulgences?
44. Mary The Mother of God
45. The Marian Cult
46. What is a Saint?
47. What is an Angel?

PART FIVE: THE LIFE OF FAITH

48. What is the Church?
49. What is a Sacrament?
50. Christian Initiation
51. Penance and Absolution
52. What is the Eucharist?
53. What is a Priest?
54. Christian Marriage
55. Death and the Christian
56. Christian Morality
57. Christian Social Teaching
58. World Morality
59. Christianity and Money

PART SIX: THE WORD OF GOD

60. What is the Bible?
61. The Promised Land
62. Biblical Archaeology
63. Biblical Criticism
64. God's People in the Bible
65. The Religion of Israel
66. The Prophets
67. How Do We Know Jesus?
68. The Life of Our Lord
69. What is the Good News?
70. St. Paul and His Message
71. What the Old Testament Does Not Tell Us
72. The New Testament Apocrypha
73. Judaism

TWENTIETH CENTURY ENCYCLOPEDIA OF CATHOLICISM

PART SEVEN: THE HISTORY OF THE CHURCH

74. Christian Beginnings
75. The Dawn of the Middle Ages
76. The Early Middle Ages
77. The Later Middle Ages
78. Reformation and Counter-Reformation
79. The Church in the Modern Age

PART EIGHT: THE ORGANIZATION OF THE CHURCH

80. What is Canon Law?
81. The Papacy
82. The Ecumenical Councils
83. Successors of the Apostles
84. The Christian Priesthood
85. Religious Orders of Men
86. Religious Orders of Women
87. The Laity's Place in the Church
88. The Catholic Spirit

PART NINE: THE CHURCH AND THE MODERN WORLD

89. Church and State
90. Christianity and Economics
91. Contemporary Atheism
92. Science and Religion
93. Christianity and Psychiatry
94. Christianity and the Machine Age
95. Christianity and the Space Age
96. Christianity and Communism
97. Christianity and Colonialism
98. The Church Works Through Her Saints
99. History of the Missions
100. Missions in the World Today
101. Religious Sociology
102. The Mission of the Church in the World
103. The Church and Sex
104. The Workers of the Church
105. Charity in Action
106. Christianity and Education
107. Why We Believe

PART TEN: THE WORSHIP OF THE CHURCH

108. The Spirit of Worship
109. The Books of Worship
110. History of the Mass
111. The Mass in the West
112. Eastern Liturgies
113. The Christian Calendar
114. Vestments and Church Furniture

PART ELEVEN: CATHOLICISM AND LITERATURE

115. What is a Christian Writer?
116. Sacred Languages
117. Christian Humanism
118. To be assigned
119. Modern Christian Literature

PART TWELVE: CATHOLICISM AND THE ARTS

120. The Christian Meaning of Art
121. The Origins of Christian Art
122. Church Building
123. Christian Painting and Sculpture
124. Christian Theatre
125. Christian Music
126. Motion Pictures, Radio and Television

PART THIRTEEN: CATHOLICISM AND SCIENCE

127. Embryo and Anima
128. Nuclear Physics in Peace and War
129. Medicine and Morals
130. To be assigned
131. To be assigned
132. To be assigned
133. To be assigned

PART FOURTEEN: OUTSIDE THE CHURCH

134. To be assigned
135. Greek and Russian Orthodoxy
136. Heresies and Heretics
137. Protestantism
138. The Ecumenical Movement
139. Modern Sects

PART FIFTEEN: NON-CHRISTIAN BELIEFS

140. Primitive Religions
141. Religions of the Ancient East
142. Greco-Roman Religion
143. Mohammedanism
144. Hinduism
145. Buddhism
146. Mystery Cults
147. Superstition
148. The Rationalists

PART SIXTEEN: GENERAL AND SUPPLEMENTARY VOLUMES

149. Why I am a Christian
150. Index

All titles are subject to change.